ROGER HILLEGAS

with **Eric Hillegas** *and* **Elaine Hillegas**

Shaping
Christian
CHARACTER

FINDING YOUR VISION,

BUILDING YOUR ENDURANCE,

RENEWING YOUR PASSION

AND KEEPING YOUR FOCUS

Published by

BOOKS YOU CAN DEPEND ON

a division of VMI Publishers
Sisters, Oregon
www.vmipublishers.com

ISBN: 1-933204-21-4
Library of Congress Control Number: 2006923898
Author Contact: regje5@gmail.com

TABLE OF CONTENTS

Elaine and I dedicate this book to our children: Greg, our eldest son, who has great vision and endurance; Julie, our daughter-in-law, the daughter that love brought; Eric, our youngest son, who lives with great passion and focus; and our daughter, Julie Marie, who left us way too soon at the age of thirteen, and though absent, she renews hope and lives on in our hearts.

ACKNOWLEDGEMENTS

A book is never published without the help and support of many people, especially an Author's first endeavor.

First and foremost I want to thank my wife Elaine, whose wisdom and support have made my ministry and book possible. Her list of talents and her enduring energy are amazing. Her heart of love and joy has been such an overwhelming blessing to me and our family as well as to many in places too numerous to mention. The insights she brought to this work, and especially to the chapters on women made this book far more meaningful. Thank you!

I want to thank my son Eric for his diligent work in transcribing my audio messages into the written word, and using his extensive education to bring special insights and understanding to the text.

I appreciate Dave Phillips' invaluable support, encouragement and help through the years of our ministry, and his special talent in finding the smallest flaw in a sentence.

I am also thankful for the support and help of VMI Publishers.

Roger Hillegas
April 21, 2006

PREFACE

I am a preacher. When speaking to congregations I usually begin with the following disclaimer:

Over the last several years I have had multiple eye surgeries for glaucoma. They didn't go well. I have lost most of my vision. Most of you (actually, all of you) sitting out there are just nebulous shadows. If you want to leave, feel free. I won't know the difference. Just don't laugh, I can't see my watch either...

It takes a while for that last one to sink in, but they usually get it.

Obviously, a reader doesn't have to worry about a long-winded preacher. However, the printed word brings its own set of challenges. How do I capture spoken messages, some of which I have shared for more than two decades, and convert them into text? More significantly, how on earth do I keep your eyes glued to a sheet of paper?

Conversing with an author, even a good one, can be tricky. Thankfully I am not an author. After years of honest effort and honest feedback, I've reached the following conclusion: God has gifted my mouth more than my pen. I have spent much of my adult life speaking to people as I wander to-and-fro on a platform. That's where my passions and gifts intersect. That's where I function best.

Why then would I raise a pen and mute my voice? Good question. The answer: I didn't. My youngest son undertook the task of his own free will. As family scribe, Eric has condensed some thoughts and expanded others. In an effort to capture my voice, he has also attempted to preserve speaking mannerisms that sometimes stretch the bounds of proper grammar. My voice is unmistakable in the text. Again, that's my strong suit. If I could find a way to include facial expressions and hand gestures, believe me, I would.

May God speak to you through the written words of a verbal pastor.

—Roger L. Hillegas

When copying ancient texts, scribes sometimes altered manuscripts to reflect personal views. As manuscripts circulated these alterations could easily be mistaken for original intent. In time, entire families of altered, even conflicting, manuscripts could supplant an author's original text. Although technological advances have removed many barriers to communication, we have found countless new ways to obscure, alter, or "spin" messages. The cycle continues.

I could certainly be accused of scribal creativity in the text before you. However, I have performed alterations under the full care and supervision of the author. In addition, I have had the privilege of literally sitting at the feet of this author for a number of years. The differences between ancient scribes and myself run deeper than method and manner, even deeper than quill and keyboard. I'm rather familiar with the messenger. He's my father.

I have taken pains to preserve my father's voice in this text. He's good. You don't make a living with your mouth unless you've been blessed with good chops. However, to make the point crystal clear, *speakin' aint writin'.* I have taken liberty to rework and rephrase parts of his message to make them more reader friendly. I have also expanded several points where I felt I had something to offer. No doubt, ancient scribes believed their alterations represented improvements every bit as much as my own. That danger goes with the territory. Hopefully, my knowledge of the messenger and his message has kept me on the straight and narrow. Failing that, my dad retained absolute veto authority.

I have tried to be my dad's best voice. I have tried to build on the foundation of his legacy. Come to think of it, that's a pretty good description of family. Thank you, dad.

—Eric M. Hillegas

1

WHAT'S YOUR VISION?

If you've done a little channel surfing recently you probably realize that infomercials are spreading. Just like waistlines and hips, they're getting harder to avoid. Infomercials are no longer relegated to irrelevant channels or late nights. You can find them any time of day on any number of channels. Both nauseating and captivating, these marketing gems provide a wonderful capacity to discover all kinds of things. If you just buy a $397 set of tapes you can become a multi-millionaire in the span of mere days. Even better, you can actually get property for free and sell it for loads of money. Isn't that wonderful? But wait…if you buy this abdominal thing you can have chiseled abs just like the guy on TV. Yeah, right.

Here's the point: we're being motivated. The motivational industry used to consist of a couple of guys who could have worked for the circus. Now it's a multi-billion dollar industry and it doesn't seem to be slowing down. Remember, it's just like waistlines and hips (they keep spreading). People are trying to reach us, to move us, to motivate us. We aren't just being offered trinkets and tools we're being offered quality of life. If we make the right purchases we can have better lives, even become better people. Be honest, you've at least thought about that ab machine.

Infomercials and marketing gimmicks strike a nerve for a reason. They are riding the coattails of proverbial truth: without a vision you perish. The Biblical rendering: "Where there is no vision, the people are unrestrained," (Prov. 29:18). Lack of restraint (i.e., self-discipline) inevitably leads to spiritual (if not physical) death. There isn't much wiggle room in that equation.

Before going any further let's clarify what we're talking about with the word "vision." In simplest terms, and throughout this discussion, vision refers to revelation. In fact, that's exactly how the NIV translates Proverbs 29:18: "Where there is no revelation, the people cast off restraint." Vision is revelation. That sharpens our understanding, but let's tighten the definition even further. For the purposes of this discussion, vision refers to a revealed picture of life at its best.

Within this overarching vision it is possible to have many smaller visions—we all do. Included in a vision of life at its best it is possible to have vision for chiseled abs, a sprawling investment portfolio, dazzling white teeth, and/or designer shoes. Each of these individual visions (revealed pictures) contributes to an overall picture of "the good life." Here's the important question: what are your controlling visions? Given the many visions we all entertain, which revelations take precedence? To raise the stakes even higher is it even necessary to maintain controlling visions? Is it better to simply assume a decidedly Western posture and privatize vision, pursuing whatever dreams strike your fancy in whatever fashion you decide? I will answer that question with an emphatic *no*, but I don't want to get too far ahead of myself.

If you have no vision, you will perish. It's pretty simple, pretty straightforward. You'd think with a principle that simple and that terminal people would have pretty sensitive "vision radar." Unfortunately, that doesn't seem to be the case. Think about what happens as people grow older and tell me if this doesn't sound familiar. As we journey through life we come to realize that youth is wasted on the young. We also realize that we were so naïve in our youth. We thought we could do anything. We had the strength of youth and we had ideas—seemingly exciting, compelling, and motivating ideas. But now we're mature. The wiles of youth have seasoned into the platitudes of maturity. Yet, from the heights of maturity we look down at the situations of life and wonder why there is no vitality. We wonder why everything seems so...dead.

Lost vision and spiritual death are the lot of all too many. Sadly, this is not a new phenomenon. Like so many patterns in life we can look to Scripture for instruction. In the chapters of Deuteronomy, before Israel even entered the Promised Land, Moses repeatedly warned the people not to lose vision. You can almost hear his tone of voice. There's a strong whiff of foreknowledge in the air. As he retraces Israel's journey with God, time and again Moses admonishes the people to diligently observe and never forget Yahweh's commands (e.g., Deut.4:6,23; 5:1,32,33; 6:3,6-9,17,25; 7:12; 8:6,11,19).

Honestly, it almost seems excessive. You wonder if the ol' boy is trying to dampen the mood. It should have been a time of eager expectation, and it was.

But it was also as if Moses knew what would happen, and it did—repeatedly. Much of Israel's story, much of the entire Old Testament is a tragically repetitive wheel: God's grace, Israel's lost vision, Israel's rebellion, God's punishment, Israel's cry for help, God's grace and redemption—you get the picture. Time and again Israel lost vision and experienced death.

Maybe Israel just didn't get it. Maybe God's message didn't connect the way it was supposed to. I mean, come on, two stone tablets aren't exactly flashy reminders of God's commandments. Let's think cutting edge. If someone can produce a twenty-minute infomercial inducing people to buy cheese graters, couldn't God have produced a better package for the Israelites? Couldn't He have sustained the vision with a little better production value?

Oh believe me, He produced the mother of all infomercials. This was infinitely more than a couple of crude stone tablets. Try this: the literal presence of God descending on Mt. Sinai in a fiery cloud (Ex. 19:9). Emanating from the cloud are thunder, lightning, a loud trumpet, and the voice of God Himself (Ex. 19:16-20). This display was so intense, so interactive that getting too close meant certain death (Ex. 19:21)! You can bet the earth was shaking, and so were the hearts of Israel:

> *All the people perceived the thunder and the lightning flashes and the sound of the trumpet and the mountain smoking; and when the people saw it, they trembled and stood at a distance. Then they said to Moses, "Speak to us yourself and we will listen; but let not God speak to us, or we will die," (Ex. 20:18-19).*

This was no B-grade production. God knew what He was doing. Indeed, He intended to put fear in the hearts of Israel to keep them from sinning (Ex. 20:20). So impressive was this display that Moses coined a new name for Israel's God: The Consuming Fire (Deut. 4:24). This name provided vivid imagery and conjured up the entire Sinai experience. It was an easy and (oh, so) powerful handle for Israel to sustain its vision.

Given that impressive display, that lasting impression, and that powerfully vivid name, how could Moses seemingly know that Israel would lose vision after entering the Promised Land? Simple, he'd seen it happen before. As we'll discuss below, the forty years prior to Israel's entrance into the Promised Land were spent wandering the wilderness for the same reason: lost vision.

Israel's persistent and pervasive loss of vision in the face of God's revelation tells us why no infomercial and no set of tapes will ever change your life, solve your problems, or make you a better person. Infomercials and marketing gimmicks may induce you to buy a new cheese grater or a fancy ab machine but the following truth remains: the human heart forgets and fails just as easily as the human mind. I am amazed that we are still so prone to think otherwise. It would be funny if it wasn't so tragic. Look, if the Israelites couldn't sustain spiritual vision after witnessing the unparalleled, unmatched works of the God of the universe (Deut. 4:32-35), don't be so naïve to think a motivational gimmick will sustain your emotional or spiritual engine. Moses could see the failure before it ever happened because he knew the human heart. "*When* you...become complacent,"—complacency as a given—"*if* you act corruptly,"—the all-too-likely result (Deut. 4:25—NRSV, italics added).

Does this mean that Israel was helpless? Was lost vision simply a foregone conclusion? Were they impotent in the face of the world, unable to pursue any course that would guard their hearts and sustain vision? Hardly.

Keep these words that I am commanding you today in your heart. Recite them to your children and talk about them when you are at home and when you are away, when you lie down and when you rise. Bind them as a sign on your hand, fix them as an emblem on your forehead, and write them on the doorposts of your house and on your gates. (Deut. 6:6-9—NIV)

It doesn't get much clearer than that. Vision is not self-sustaining, but it can be guarded. This world chews up and spits out visions at an alarming rate. No vision is strong enough to withstand the assaults of our world. Vision must be fostered and it must be sustained. Without persistent effort, vision dies. Here is a foundational principle: sustained vision demands battle of the will.

Without a vision, you perish. I hope you grasp the importance of this equation. It is true for individuals, and it is profoundly true for the church. I'm not alone in this message. Lots of people will tell you that spiritual vision is the key to life, love, and happiness. We don't have a shortage of vision-casters. To the contrary, we have a glut of so-called visionaries crowding the airwaves. Vision is critical but the message is dangerously incomplete if simply left at the stage of "spiritual vision." Once you've grasped the importance of vision, you've only just begun the journey. Just any vision won't do.

Human flourishing demands more than messages from marketers and motivators. I'll warn you right now, there are countless rabbit trails on this journey. Just like watches and cologne, some of the knockoffs look and smell pretty good. However, if you let yourself be captured by the latest vision to roll out the door, your life will be the sad tale of an artificially inflated and wholly underdeveloped spirit. You will forever be caught in the changing tide, forever finding new ways to paint a smile on your face and explain the latest secret to happiness. None of these solutions will last. That's not the way the system works. Marketing demands change. Without change the industry dies. If you're not convinced, start channel surfing again and you'll see what I mean.

This spiritual journey demands concentrated attention in the right direction. The critical question isn't, "Do you have a vision?" The critical question is, "What is your vision?" All roads don't lead to heaven. Human flourishing is not just a private affair that can be approached the same way you select your daily attire. These are strong claims but they are foundational for everything that follows. Misguided motivation is not only wasted effort it's downright dangerous. You're probably saying to yourself, "Okay, so what's the answer?" Scripture, the Word, God. Rather than submitting to motivators of the day, we need to recognize God's revealed, unchanging design in the matter.

For more than twenty-five years I have spent my weekends traveling the globe and speaking at various churches. As you might imagine, I have nearly mastered the art of packing. Here's some good advice from a seasoned traveler: always pack your toiletries (maybe even some fresh underclothes) in your carry-on bag. You only have to endure the pain of lost luggage once for this lesson to sink in.

In addition to luggage, I have carried the concept of character development across the globe. That's what I do. I teach about character. Specifically, I look at character development through the lens of gender, considering what gender entails in our growth as men and women of God. I am amazed at the number of ways we misinterpret, misunderstand, or downright underestimate our gender. Gender goes much deeper than issues of marriage or procreation. You wouldn't guess as much from a survey of pop culture - but then again pop culture isn't the only place where gender is marginalized. I have actually heard gender diminished in the hallowed halls of church. Bible-believing Christians refer to passages that in the resurrection none "marry nor are given in marriage." (Matt. 22:30). As a result they feel rather high-minded when they adopt an asexual attitude toward spiritual matters. Gender is just glossed over as something to put up with during this life.

I agree that in the resurrection none will marry nor be given in marriage, but here's the secret of that little passage: the resurrection hasn't happened yet. I don't care how much you like your hometown. I don't care if you think paradise is nothing more than palm trees and pineapples. Let me break it down for you: the resurrection hasn't happened and this isn't the new heavens and the new earth. As long as we are in these tents of clay, these either male or female bodies, something unique is working in us to produce different choices, different changes, and different growth curves. The way we think, the way we deal with life, the way we handle our thoughts, idiosyncrasies, responsibilities, and concerns are largely predicated upon our gender. Our gender is fundamentally responsible for the way we view and deal with life.

Through the context of gender we will make choices. The culmination of those choices produces our eternal character. Yes, the body will die and return to dust but the promise of resurrection life awaits. We are not awaiting a disembodied future. Scripture indicates that we will actually be more fully clothed in the life to come (2Cor. 5:4). We are waiting for new bodies that neither decay nor die. Resurrection life is shrouded in mystery but regardless of the details, our character in resurrection life will have been greatly impacted by the housing, the body, which characterizes this time of life. As we sit here today, human bodies only come in two flavors: male and female. As men and women of God who desire to rule and reign with Him for eternity, it is therefore not only a good idea, but incumbent upon us to recognize how this clay mold affects our thoughts, our choices, and our journeys.

How do we evolve spiritually with respect to our gender? The world has brought incredible frustration and confusion in answer to this question. Let's start back in the 1960's. It's safe to say that Western culture was in a rather rebellious mood in the days of hippies and flower power. We threw everything up in the air. We thought God was dead and we had a new morality (which was neither new, nor moral). Simply put, we could make our own rules and act however we wanted. In the midst of this movement, one concept took off like wildfire: unisex. In efforts to surpass the constraints of gender, both genders dressed alike and wore long hair, and neither gender used deodorant. For the most part, we were flagrantly violating God-given parameters for identity and character development (cf. Rom. 1:18-32). It shouldn't have come as a surprise that we generated some real confusion about gender.

You'd go out with friends. Someone would point to a person over in the corner and ask, "What do you think that is over there?" You'd reply, "I don't know, but you'd better not touch it!" Common sense went completely out the window. You just couldn't be sure what was intrinsically male or female. As a result you started to question what was distinctive or useful about gender. Were gender distinctions even valid? Maybe it was just a matter of plumbing. In the 1970's and the 1980's we recovered some gender distinctions, especially with respect to the way we dressed. Then all of a sudden we started hearing about sexual preference. We heard the gospels of choice and pluralism. Once again we were thrown for a loop by the ways of the world. There was a constant and ever-growing tendency to look at things—everything!—from new, different, or supposedly more developed perspectives. In this context the absolutes of Scripture looked very different.

You see, the world is constantly telling us that there are no absolutes—and of that they are absolutely sure. The mentality of the age is so seductive because it appears oh, so supportive, and oh, so affirming. Personal redemption means no longer having to obey anyone or anything. "Whatever you want to do, baby, do it." Appropriate action and inclusiveness are the orders of the day. Just follow your best feelings. If you think you're a good person, then you are good. To support this agenda, we've adapted our entire vocabulary.

Don't you get a kick out of political correctness? I recently heard somebody who was rather upset. He said he no longer wanted to be known as "short." He was just "vertically challenged." I said, "I can accept that. Some mornings I wake up feeling horizontally challenged." Somebody else piped in, "No, no, no. You're just nutritionally enriched." I said, "Isn't that nice!" Then, I looked in the mirror one morning and cried, "Oh, no! I'm follicly deficient."

Here's the point. If your hair is gone, that's truth. If you can grow more hair in your ears and on your back than you can on your forehead, you're bald. Get over it. I don't care what you call it, truth wins. Labels must conform to truth, not the other way around. You can change labels every week of the year, you can dress them up as much as you'd like, but eventually they will come to reflect existing attitudes towards truth. I'm not giving anyone permission to be rude or insensitive. Our speech should always be seasoned with grace (Col. 4:6), but that seasoning is not reducible to a changing label. You will never effect lasting change by massaging attitudes with vocabulary. Terminology, whatever it is, becomes negative or positive depending on prevailing attitudes toward truth. You simply can't play games in that arena. Truth wins out over political correctness every time.

How does this relate to gender? It is fundamentally important for us to recognize that God has made us uniquely men and women. That is truth, and that is good. He has utilized gender for a purpose. The human body literally adds shape and form to our character development. The body is a character perfecter. Our season of life in this tent of clay may be temporary, but it is purposeful and it is powerful. The results will endure.

Before I start talking about gender specifics, let me make a few disclaimers. First, these are the observations of a preacher, not a psychologist. However, I believe they are very consistent with Biblical wisdom and the broader Christian worldview. I have shared these observations for more than twenty-five years with tens of thousands of people across the globe and I have yet to be informed that I'm downright nuts. To the contrary, the resonance has been very strong.

Second, I am dealing with broad categories. Obviously, the traits I describe are not entirely restricted to one gender or the other. Rather, I am dealing with some of the strongest God-given tendencies of each gender. For instance, it's not that men value achievement and women don't. We both value achievement. However, men tend to view accomplishment and achievement as primary motivators—sources of identity. For women, things often look a bit different. More than a source of identity, women tend to view achievement as a source of security. As I will describe in fuller detail, it's a simple matter of the female heart (security-oriented) versus the male eye (achievement-oriented).

This leads to another disclaimer: you don't have to look very far to find women who display what I term "male" tendencies or vice versa. Some folks argue that such overlap invalidates gender differences and proves the culturally conditioned nature of gender. I disagree. Overlap should not be surprising and it certainly doesn't invalidate inherent gender distinctions. In fact, it would be more surprising if overlap or understanding were completely absent. That's the beauty of God's design: mutuality. We are both made in God's image (Gen. 1:27). As such, overlap also does not mean that someone is being a "bad man" or a "bad woman" if their tendency profile fluctuates across the spectrum.

Finally, I recognize that some issues speak very strongly to both genders but I may highlight these issues within the context of a specific gender. In sum, gender is a God-given instrument, characterized by consistent tendencies. To the extent we understand these tendencies we will have greater insight into the unique challenges of our character development as men and women of God. However, I would never presume to reduce gender to a simple formula. These disclaimers are surely imperfect (unsatisfactory for some and inflammatory for others) but they provide a meaningful and altogether reasonable foundation for the following discussion.

2

VISION AND A MAN'S EYE: ACHIEVEMENT AND ENVY

Then the sons of Judah drew near to Joshua in Gilgal, and Caleb the son of Jephunneh the Kenizzite said to him, "You know the word which the LORD spoke to Moses the man of God concerning you and me in Kadesh-barnea. I was forty years old when Moses the servant of the LORD sent me from Kadesh-barnea to spy out the land, and I brought word back to him as it was in my heart. Nevertheless my brethren who went up with me made the heart of the people melt with fear; but I followed the LORD my God fully. So Moses swore on that day, saying, 'Surely the land on which your foot has trodden will be an inheritance to you and to your children forever, because you have followed the LORD my God fully.'"

~ Joshua 14:6-9

Men, let's look at some of our distinguishing traits. We are basically visually and externally oriented. We generally deal from the outward, motivated by and responding to external realities. As such, men tend to gain their value and their sense of identity from accomplishment: the big house, the beautiful wife, the two-and-a-half kids, the dog named Spot, the big car, the wonderful title, the great job—"What a *maaan!*" Being visually oriented, men are also visually sexually stimulated. Madison Avenue has understood this for decades: "How many times can we get the bikini in the beer commercial?" Sex sells.

This predominantly visual and external orientation has produced certain abilities. For instance, men have the capacity to accurately evaluate themselves. We tend to know how well we can accomplish things. Being visual, being external, dealing with the outward, it's pretty natural for us to observe data, crunch a few calculations, and produce an assessment. We don't even have to think about it. This particular process is not only intuitive, it's also the closest many men ever get to cooking.

Men tend to accurately assess their resources and abilities. This tendency is woven into our very fiber. It can even border on compulsion. We are so confident in our ability to accurately assess that we feel perfectly comfortable extending it to others. Let me suggest a little experiment. Next January, see how many guys you can find who don't have an opinion about which team is going to win the Superbowl. I'm serious. Some guys may feign indifference or act reluctant, but if you're genuinely interested most guys will tell you what's really going to happen. It doesn't matter if they've extensively researched the issue or not. If a guy knows anything about the game of football, he's got an opinion because he's already run the numbers. It's woven into our fabric.

It doesn't have to be football. Take any sport. If a guy plays golf, he still knows what I mean. This typical male tendency goes deeper than knowing which club to select from a certain distance in the fairway. It's more subtle, more pervasive. It looks more like this. When a guy walks up to the tee with a bag full of golf balls, he'll whip out his driver without blanching. However, if you really want to see what he thinks about his game, watch that same guy approach the tee with a depleted bag of balls. If he's actually "got game" he'll still whip out that driver. If he doesn't, he already knows it and you'll see him downgrade to a three wood or something less risky. Even if a guy isn't involved in sports he'll probably know how well he could perform if his body hadn't gone to pot, or whatever. Again, the point is simply this: men accurately assess and intuitively know their abilities.

There's a problem, though. Guys aren't always real honest when sharing their assessment with others. I don't mean that we flat-out lie, we just stick to the highlights. It's a very simple recipe: one part ego, one part accomplishment, one part external orientation (like I said, this is how most guys cook). Mix all three together and you end up with something that seems perfectly natural to the male mind: you only tell 'em what's best about yourself.

Guys know this syndrome. You want to make yourself look a little better than you actually are. We got this here ego to protect so we just share our good points. If you've gone out and played golf and you've lost a lot of golf balls and killed a whole bunch of worms, yet you had a couple of good shots—*pshoong*, right down the fairway—then those are the ones you remember. Those are the ones you tell everybody about. Those are the ones that come up the next day at work when you're shooting the breeze around the water cooler.

"Did you play yesterday?"

"Oh, yeah."

"How was your—"

"*Pshoong*, right down the middle of the fairway!"

This affinity for polishing our performance and making ourselves look better might feel natural, but danger is always lurking around the corner. What if the company golf champion walks up right about then and says, "Oh, really? You're getting good, huh? Let's go out and play." Now you've been called out! Now someone—everyone!—is gonna find out that basically you're still killing worms. That, "down the middle of the fairway," business was just a lucky fluke.

Sensing imminent danger, your ego kicks into overdrive. We need defense mechanisms—stat! The objectives are clear and compelling: avoid being exposed and save face in the process. The ego must be defended at all costs. What's the typical solution to this achievement-oriented pressure cooker? Withdrawal: physically, emotionally, and spiritually. When our ego gets threatened we find inner clarity real quick. The guy who seemed so bold suddenly turns in full retreat. "I'm outta here! I'm not gonna let everybody kick me around." We pull back. Suddenly we remember that our hip went out on us. "You know, on that last hole something funny happened with my knee and hip. I don't know if I can play this weekend." We pull back.

Nature abhors a vacuum. As soon as we pull back in order to save face, to avoid being exposed for that all too generous self-evaluation, someone else will fill the void. Some young guy who's only kicked around a few balls at the driving range will step up to the company champ and say, "Hey, I'll go play with you if he doesn't want to play. I can use all the help I can get." Suddenly, someone else is right where we wish we could have been. Before long, this kid who couldn't even swing straight is becoming pretty good because he's getting all kinds of tips from the company champ. And that's when a powerful emotion begins welling up within: envy. Other people are gaining what should have been ours. Remember, we're visually oriented. Envy connotes the eye. When you see others gaining what should have been yours, when that feeling simmers and boils within, your vision will die. Envy kills vision. Disappointment will border on rage. "How come I didn't get that?! That opportunity should have been mine!" Frustration and envy spread like wildfire, consuming as they go. A fertile soul is reduced to wasteland in the blink of an eye. When that happens, you simply cannot accommodate (let alone sustain) spiritual vision.

It is incumbent for us guys to know our vision. What is your vision? What vision do you have for your wife? Don't succumb to the danger of indifference.

Don't fall prey to pleasure. Don't you dare set up camp in the vast field of comfort. The rhythms of life breed familiarity and complacency. Remember the words of Moses, "When you...become complacent," (Deut. 4:25). It becomes easier to settle. You start to think, "I don't need much more—just the family. Let the little woman do her thing." No! No! No! What vision do you have to see this woman become all that God purposes? If you have no vision, or the wrong vision, then try to imagine standing before the God who says, "That woman would have been better off if I had killed you in your crib." What vision do you have for your wife? If you are truly one flesh, her accomplishments will be your accomplishments. To state it differently, what she accomplishes is what you will become. So many times I see men denigrate or belittle their wives. That is utterly foolish. I want to walk right up and say, "You're putting yourself down. You're degrading your own flesh."

What vision do you have for your wife? What vision do you have for your children? Do you say things like, "Ah, kids got it so easy today. You know, back when I was young we had to walk nine miles uphill both ways to school. The snow was this deep." Yeah right, you probably grew up in Florida.

Do you see it? That's nothing but envy. It's nothing more than scornful words and petty complaining. "You know this younger generation, they've got PC's, iPods, and Nike Air. I never had a Nike nothing!" Envy. It happens so easily. Yet, isn't it amazing that God has called us to elevate our children, to allow our children to stand on our shoulders so they might accomplish more than we ever dreamed? That is a controlling vision that secures honor. It is profoundly important for us to realize these principles.

Like most men, I distinctly remember reaching the threshold of manhood. In our culture, it happens at the ripe old age of eighteen or nineteen. You know, right when you're supposed to call upon all of your accumulated wisdom to decide what you want to do for the next fifty years. I was raised in a pastor's home. I didn't know whether I wanted to go into the ministry, but I did know that I liked the TV show *Perry Mason*. The courtroom adventures of this brilliant attorney were all the rage during the 1960's. I distinctly remember wanting to stand in front of a jury and yell, "Objection your honor. Irrelevant! Immaterial!" I thought I could do that really well. Then, some dear saint at church mentioned that it was impossible to be a lawyer and a Christian at the same time. Now, with forty years of hindsight I'm beginning to wonder whether you can be a minister and a Christian at the same time (I'm kidding...mostly).

That dear old saint was no prophet. Unfortunately, her statement reflected more about our particular corner of church than it reflected about God's truth. It reflected a church that was becoming increasingly insular. We were losing vision. We were becoming so heavenly minded that we were no earthly good. We were beginning to withdraw. We had no vision.

You remember what happens when we withdraw. Something else will fill the void. The humanists, and the agnostics, and the "isms", and the cults, and the various religions of the world filled the voids left by the church. In Washington, DC, and in state capitols, and in city halls, and in the corporate and educational boardrooms of this nation they filled the void. Now all of a sudden, if you're a Christian you're thought of as a right-wing whacko. All of a sudden, one of the few groups that can be legally discriminated against is Christians. It's our own fault, because the church withdrew. If we're going to reclaim the high ground, it's going to be through our children.

What is your vision?

We recognized that our youngest son was very gifted. He was one of those well-rounded individuals who could do all things well. I remember thinking, "What if I had a mentally or physically handicapped child?" What would I have done? I'll tell you what I would have done. I would have searched for the very best teachers and the very best trainers I could possibly find so that, whatever his limitations, my son could have achieved his maximum potential. So if I discover ability rather than handicap, why wouldn't I likewise do everything possible to ensure my son's flourishing? God allowed our son to go to Notre Dame. He graduated summa cum laude—twice. Those achievements opened doors. They made things possible. However, opportunities and possibilities have never been the greatest joy. The greatest joy has been watching his abilities grow and flourish.

I say to you, fathers, you have to pay the price. You can't just say, "Oh it would be nice if..." You have to pay the price. If you have a vision, you're going to do what is necessary to help that child, to help your wife, to find a place where that vision can be fulfilled. It is incumbent upon us as men of God to have a vision for our family, to have a vision for God to utilize them to their highest ability and to our highest honor.

What vision do you have for your church?

"Well, you know, it's the pastor, it's the staff—they have the vision." Yes, as shepherds of Christ's Church, your pastor and church leaders should have a vision. But they shouldn't be alone. Your church is a body. It's not just a head. If your church was just a head, it would look real funny rolling around on the ground. It's a body fit jointly together. Obviously, if you're a part of this body and you have no vision, you're like a dead arm. The head keeps saying, "C'mon arm, get with it!" Or, if you're an arm that's got your own vision not fit jointly with the head, then you're a wild, spurious arm and the head is forever saying, "Settle down, arm!"

What is your vision?

Do you have a vision to see God utilize you in your church? Do you have a vision to be a part of God's Kingdom, serving its needs and fulfilling God's desire? God does not bless us so that we can feel good. Blessedness is not simple happiness (Matt 5:3-12). God blesses so that we can occupy the land and reveal His glory. Without a vision, you perish.

I am utterly amazed by Caleb, the man referenced at the beginning of this chapter. I don't know whether you need to make appointments in heaven, but I sure want to talk with this guy. We first meet Caleb out in the desert. We meet him after Moses confronted Pharaoh, after Moses relayed Yahweh's command to let the people go, after Pharaoh said, "Fat chance," and after the galactic duel between Yahweh and the gods of Egypt. After the Exodus and onto the wilderness—that's where we meet Caleb. Along with Joshua, he is one of the leaders of the twelve tribes. Caleb is about forty years old when we meet him, and from the get-go he is a prominent figure.

The Biblical story of God's people to this point has built steadily towards a climax. After promises, blessings, betrayal, redemption, and slavery, the nation of Israel has reached the shore of the Jordan. They are literally on the cusp of their God-given inheritance: Canaan. Egypt, the plagues, and the Red Sea are all behind them. The big moment has finally arrived.

Now, let's think about this. For 430 years they have had a vision to return to Canaan, to bring the bones of Joseph back to the land flowing with milk and honey, back to the land of Abraham and Isaac and Jacob. That's been their consuming vision for 430 years—and there it is! It's just across the river. "Yes! We're the generation that sees it!" What could possibly go wrong? This haunting adage: you are most susceptible to your greatest failures immediately following your greatest success. That is the sad story of the book of Numbers. Let's take a look.

This was it! Canaan, the Promised Land! The Israelites send over twelve spies from the twelve tribes. A few weeks later they come back and report to Moses. Eager to hear the report, the people ask, "What's it like over there?" The spies respond, "Oh, it's incredible! Pomegranates are THIS BIG. It takes two guys with a stick just to carry a cluster of grapes. But, there are giants over there. Those dudes are nine and ten feet tall. We look like ants in their sight. You know what? This is a wonderful place over here on this side of the river. Let's just stay right here. We'll leave Canaan to the giants."

But Caleb comes through. Caleb is the one who quiets the nay-sayers. Caleb is the one who says, "Let's roll! Right now! We will overcome!" The nay-sayers don't buy in. What's more, they take their message to the people, reporting gloom and doom in the streets—and the people buy it. "Oh, no! We've come all this way to die! If we go in there we'll get flattened and our children will be nothing but booty. Let's go back to Egypt!"

Again, Caleb steps up to defend the vision. This time Joshua joins him. "Don't you remember the mountain of God? Don't you remember the ten plagues? Don't you remember the Red Sea with Pharaoh's army bobbing up-and-down like apples? Remember all that God has done. Remember our Consuming Fire! He is surely with us and those giants will be our bread. We can do it!"

Too late. The people's heart had already melted with fear. In an amazing moment the glory of God, The Consuming Fire, again descends and speaks to Moses. "How long will these people refuse to believe me?! After all the signs I have done? Moses, I'm just gonna wipe 'em all out and give you a new nation." "No, God! If you do that the Egyptians will hear about it and spread the news all over the land. Instead, show your power by your forgiveness."

God relents, but justice is served. None of those who witnessed the Consuming Fire of Egypt and Sinai will enter the Promised Land. Moses reports the words of God. "All of you who are twenty years of age and older are going to wander in this place you so dearly wanted: the wilderness. Within forty years you're all going to die off. All of you who are younger than twenty will wander for forty years and then you will enter the Promised Land...along with my faithful servants, Caleb and Joshua."

Vindication, but oh what a cost. How do you think Caleb felt? How would you have felt? "Now wait a second! You see, God, I got on a white hat. I'm one of the good guys here. I voted 'yes.' Why don't you just give me a little condo down by the Jordan and I'll wait until all these turkeys die off. I mean, it's really tough to soar with eagles when you gotta wander with turkeys—forty years?!"

Men, here is one of the keys to seeing vision fulfilled. You have to be willing to put up with the failures of others. You will never see your vision fulfilled if you let the failures of others destroy you. At this point, some of you might be thinking, "You know, I could have probably made it in the ministry. I could teach as good as this idiot. I could've made it if it hadn't been for that guy who failed back there...if I hadn't married that woman...if we hadn't had this financial problem...if this situation hadn't happened!"

So many times we blame the bad outcomes on somebody or something else. Listen to me, you are never going to see your vision fulfilled if you indulge in pity because of the failures of others. For forty years Caleb had to wander a wilderness that he didn't choose. He was faithful at the critical moment. He had said, "Yes! We can do it!" But he came up ten votes short. He had to wander because others blew it.

That could give you a real attitude problem, couldn't it? Every morning the people had to scoop up their manna, except on Friday when manna had a shelf-life of forty-eight hours instead of twenty-four. What happens if you scoop a little too deep and get sand inside your manna bowl? You'd have crunchy manna all day long. That's a recipe for an attitude problem if I ever heard one. And see, Caleb also knew that he was waiting for all these people to die off. So he'd go out for a walk in the camp and he'd see somebody and think, "Aren't you dead yet? Would you please just die?!" Forty years.

Then four decades later he stands in front of Joshua, the man who followed his lead, seemingly the man whom he had trained. Think about that. We can get really ticked-off and envious if people don't recognize how good we are. You can lose vision for a company real quick if you've invested ten or twelve years of your life, if you're qualified for a promotion and they suddenly bring in a new ninety-day wonder. Not only that, but you trained wonder boy, taught him everything he knows, and then he gets your promotion. Whoa. "Why this stupid company!" You don't like that one bit.

How do you think Caleb must have felt as the years began to pass and the leadership shifted? First it was Moses and Aaron. Then it was Moses, Aaron, and Joshua. Then it was Moses and Joshua. Then one night, God gave Joshua all of the favor that Moses accumulated in forty years of leadership (Deut. 34:9). All of this, and Caleb was still in the same spot. He was still leader of his tribe, but he was passed over by Joshua.

Joshua was a good man. He was faithful to Yahweh. But at the defining moment, when the spies brought their report from Canaan, it was Caleb who was identified for his faithfulness. Moreover, it was Caleb who the Lord commended when speaking to Moses: "My servant Caleb has a different spirit and has followed me wholeheartedly," (Num. 14:24—NIV). At the critical moment of faithfulness, we read nothing so remarkable about Joshua. Joshua is more like Caleb's sidekick. Joshua is Tonto, Caleb is the Lone Ranger. Joshua is R2-D2, Caleb is Luke Skywalker. Joshua is Robin, Caleb is Batman. You get the picture.

A lot of times we become very angry when it seems like God (let alone other people) doesn't recognize how much we have to offer. "If people would just see—," and the envy begins to kill us. We lose vision for our vocation, we lose vision for our family, we lose vision for the church. In short, we lose vision for all of the God-given opportunities before us.

I have often heard it said that the number one phobia is fear of public speaking. It's not fear of failure. It's not fear of the dark. It's not even fear of death. It's fear of public speaking. Men, what do you do when you get involved (i.e., lead) at church? You "speak" publicly: you sing, you dance, you play the trombone, you do something publicly. Consequently, most of us never step into the spotlight. So what? So, you end up at church as a warm body, and you make sure to give your offering. Before long you feel a little bit useless. A little while longer and you lose vision altogether. "They don't appreciate me down there. They elected that guy to the position I wanted. He can't even chew gum and walk at the same time!" Envy. Pretty soon you say, "I'll just stay at home and watch the preacher on TV. You can sit around in your T-shirt and burp whenever you want when you're at home. You don't even have to get all dressed up." Suddenly you're no longer at church because you've lost your vision. For forty years Caleb wandered in a wilderness that he didn't choose. Then, he was passed over for a man who seemingly followed his lead at the crucial moment.

Our responsibility is discipleship. We are called to become disciples and to disciple others. The Great Commission is not, "Go therefore and make revival." The Great Commission is, "Go therefore and make disciples," (Matt. 28:19). God has blessed you. He has given those blessings to establish His Kingdom, not just to make you feel good. What is your vision?

After forty years of wandering, Israel enters Canaan. They battle. They occupy. As the land is divided Caleb stands before Joshua, the man promoted ahead of him.

Now behold, the LORD has let me live, just as He spoke, these forty-five years, from the time that the LORD spoke this word to Moses, when Israel walked in the wilderness; and now behold, I am eighty-five years old today. I am still as strong today as I was in the day Moses sent me; as my strength

was then, so my strength is now, for war and for going out and coming in,
(Josh. 14:10-11).

Wow! What kept him? A vision. Caleb had seen the land, tasted its very fruit. Moreover, God had promised the land as an inheritance. For more than forty years, every time the manna was crunchy, every time somebody didn't die, every time the cloud moved and he wanted to do something else, Caleb remembered that place. The vision preserved him. He was still as strong, still as capable, because he still had the vision.

We hear the ol' phrase, "Beauty is only skin deep." Never forget the corollary, "Ugly is all the way through." It's fascinating what can happen when you enter the presence of an elderly person who has kept their vision fixed on God even though their body has broken down. You walk out saying, "Wow! I went to try and serve them, but what a privilege just to be in the Spirit of the Lord around them." Then you see another senior who's as strong as a horse and you think, "Whoa, they are so negative. All they talk about is how they got cheated over here and cheated over there." There is nothing more ugly than a bitter elderly person, because they've lost vision.

God desires to work His good pleasure in us. In order for that to happen, we need to learn the right lessons. Yes, sometimes people are going to cheat us. Yes, other people are going to get the breaks that we didn't get. Yes, there will surely be delays. But think of this: Caleb lost forty of the best years of his life. Don't kid yourself by saying, "Yeah, but they lived a long time back then. He lives to be over 120 years old." I don't care. Look, from forty to eighty has to be better than eighty to one-hundred-and-twenty. Don't you think? I mean things start falling off after sixty—it's just bad. He lost forty of the prime years of his life because of others. Yet, he never lost the vision.

That brings us to the next little point. On the day in question, Caleb is eighty-five years old. Think about that. He was forty when they started and we know they wandered for forty, so where did the other five years come from?" As you can probably imagine, the Canaanites didn't just roll over and give Israel the land. Caleb and the rest of the people had to kick out the overgrown pagans who had scared them off forty years earlier. Wars take time, and they exact a cost. Here's how those five years were spent: warring to establish the land. Ha! This guy was over eighty years old. Can you imagine some actuarial chart listing the life-expectancy of an eighty-year-old guy on a hand-to-hand battlefield? It's got to be about three or four seconds.

Caleb is one of only two leaders left from the years of slavery in Egypt. If we were in his shoes we could easily have demanded our rights. "Me first! Seniority." Israel was a nation of tribes, not individuals. Caleb fought the battles of his own tribe, and he faithfully fought the battles of other tribes as well. Caleb knew what was required if he was going to establish his tribe in the land where he had walked, if he was going to see the vision fulfilled. Some of you might say, "Everyone else has it so easy. Why should I put up with—?" Envy. If you won't fight the battles of others for the sake of the vision, if you won't see them trained, if you won't invest and give and pray and protect, then you will never be strong enough to see your vision accomplished. Sometimes we have to fight the battles of others.

Here he is, an eighty-five year old man, standing in front of the individual who should have followed him. In the twelfth verse of the fourteenth chapter of the book of Joshua he says, "Now then, give me this hill country about which the LORD spoke on that day, for you heard on that day that Anakim were there, with great fortified cities; perhaps the LORD will be with me, and I will drive them out as the Lord has spoken."

Ha! Obviously the ol' boy has been out in the sun a tad too long without a helmet. I mean, he's eighty-five years old and he wants to take on the hill country where the Anakim (the giants) live in their great fortified cities?! Yeah, right. I've never been in the military but it's pretty obvious that if you're up there and I'm down here, you can roll a rock down on me a whole lot easier than I can roll a rock up on you. Right? He wants to take on hills...with giants...in fortified cities. Senile? No! He kept the vision.

Being visually oriented, being driven by accomplishment, men can be incredibly envious about the breaks they didn't get. "You know if my dad hadn't...If I would have just been in that church...If I could have just gone to that school...If my folks hadn't had their divorce...If this hadn't happened to me." Don't you ever forget: everybody has giants, everybody has hills, everybody has fortified cities to deal with. Everybody. That's not the issue. The issue is: what is your vision?

A few years ago I was speaking at a church after going through my second of (eventually) five eye surgeries. I was sharing about the challenge of the surgery. When you have eye surgery for glaucoma they drill a tiny vent in your eye and drain the fluid. It's a pretty sweet deal, but the recovery is a bear. You are not allowed to bend, lift or strain for the next four-to-six weeks. If you violate this little maxim your entire eyeball can collapse, leaving a gaping hole after they remove your eye. Now, when you can't bend over to pick up a piece of paper or tie your shoes, you also can't travel. If I don't travel, we don't eat. That was a challenge. That was a test of faith. After surviving that challenge and passing that test, I shared about the ordeal while speaking at this particular church. You know, I was talking about what a wonderful patient I was, and how I was so willing to endure everything...Okay, so my wife might have a different story. The point is that I publicly shared about my struggle.

After the sermon a woman approached me. She was in her forties, and I mention her age for a reason. She was crying. She said, "I'm so thankful you shared about your eyes. I didn't realize that people like you had problems like that." If she had been ten years old I would have probably patted her on the head and said, "Thank you. Lord bless you." But I looked at this woman and said, "People like who and problems like what?" She said, "You know, those people who stand up in front like you. I didn't know you had problems." I said, "You gotta be kidding me." She replied, "No, I'm serious. I just thought God gave you special dispensation."

Whether or not you've ever had those thoughts about public figures, this is an easy trap for both men and women to fall into (as the story demonstrates). It's easy to look around and see others as the chosen ones. It's easy to look at people and think, "Boy, did they ever get the breaks. God never dealt with me that easily. How come I've always had this problem?" I repeat: everybody has hills, everybody has giants, everybody has fortified cities. The question is: what is your vision?

Which tribe did Caleb lead? "Then the sons of Judah drew near to Joshua in Gilgal," (Josh. 14:6). We hardly ever remember that fact. Caleb gave us the land of Judah. In the hills that could have been such obstacles they built a city, and they named it Jerusalem, the City of God. You're building something in your hills, gentlemen. You're building something in the struggles you deal with. Are you willing to allow God to work in it?

In 1 Peter 5:5-6 we read, "You younger men, likewise, be subject to your elders; and all of you, clothe yourselves with humility toward one another, for 'God is opposed to the proud, but gives grace to the humble.' Therefore humble yourselves under the mighty hand of God, that He may exalt you at the proper time." We men who (preferably) want it done yesterday, we men who want to do everything by ourselves and look really macho, we have been called by God to humble ourselves and accept the will of another. This posture puts everything in its proper light. When you humble yourself before God you accept His will.

Likewise, when you seek the highest good of your wife and children, you humble yourself to see the will of God accomplished.

The whole process of humility, the whole reason we adopt and sustain God's vision is that God might use us. We do it so that God might be able to work great things in our lives. I challenge you, don't lose your vision. Write it on your hearts and write it on your doorposts. Without it, you perish.

3

VISION AND A WOMAN'S HEART: SECURITY AND JEALOUSY

Now it came about in the days when the judges governed, that there was a famine in the land. And a certain man of Bethlehem in Judah went to sojourn in the land of Moab with his wife and his two sons. The name of the man was Elimelech, and the name of his wife, Naomi; and the names of his two sons were Mahlon and Chilion, Ephrathites of Bethlehem in Judah. Now they entered the land of Moab and remained there. Then Elimelech, Naomi's husband, died; and she was left with her two sons. They took for themselves Moabite women as wives; the name of the one was Orpah and the name of the other Ruth. And they lived there about ten years. Then both Mahlon and Chilion also died, and the woman was bereft of her two children and her husband.

~ Ruth 1:1-5

We have established this much so far: vision is a powerful force. Vision leads, vision directs, and vision motivates. It is elemental to human flourishing. Vision is water, and it is food. Vision sustains spiritual life but vision is not self-sustaining. Any vision can die—even God's vision for His people. Much like physical food, spiritual sustenance can spoil. The frailty of the human heart renders any vision a tenuous prospect. In the spiritual realm there is no Twinkie, no magic bullet with unending shelf-life. Vision must be vigorously protected and intentionally sustained. It must be kept fresh. Despite powerful revelations, repeated commands, and evocative reminders, God's vision requires consistent sustenance or spiritual ruin ensues. Israel sadly illustrates this principle time-and-again in the pages of the Old Testament.

Our souls hunger for God's revelation—the only reliable vision, as disclosed in Scripture—but this life holds countless distractions. Situations evolve and we are inevitably pulled along by the surging tide. Afflictions arise and we look for a quick fix. We replace theology with therapy. When it comes to God's vision for character development, we quite literally "lose it." The trials of life overwhelm therapeutic measures, allowing self-pity, anger, and despair to supplant vision. Once this cycle begins, bitterness is just around the proverbial bend.

Both genders are engaged in the struggle for sustained vision. Both genders engage common battles along the way. However in addition to the common battles, our God-given design either as male or as female will create gender-specific challenges. To the extent we understand the design of gender, we are better positioned to develop godly character.

Ladies, you operate from the heart. Where males function from an external and predominantly visual orientation, females are inward. Females are built inwardly and deal inwardly. Where males are driven by achievement, females find anchor in security. Males are motivated by accomplishment, by what they might become. Nurturing is a powerful female tendency. Men say stuff like, "What can make this thing fly?" Women ask, "Why do you want it to fly? What are you after?" Where males are visually sexually oriented, women are more romantically stimulated. Men, be very thankful that women are not primarily visually sexually oriented. Think about that for a moment and you'll figure it out. As the male body ages it can take on the appearance of a beached whale. Thank God that He allowed women to be romantically stimulated. Appearance is critically important to men, women respond to motive more than appearance. Most women see through outward appearance. How they are treated becomes very important.

Children demonstrate these tendencies with striking clarity. Guys start loitering around the monkey bars no later than junior high school. You'll hear profound statements like, "Whoa, what a babe!" If she only needed her physical beauty praised, that sort of statement would be enough. But it's not enough, not by a long shot. I don't care what you see in magazines and movies, any little girl can tell any little boy, "I am more than a body! I am a mind and I am a spirit. Treat me as a whole person." All of a sudden "little boy" is awakened to a shocking reality. He can't quite explain it, but there seems to be a mysterious depth behind the physical beauty. Fascinating, and confusing. "Little boy" would have been satisfied with the beauty (appearance), but this inexplicable and altogether unexpected depth demands something more. All of a sudden, girls are complicated. As "little boy" gets older he musters unknown resources and works real hard to demonstrate good motives: the cards, the flowers, the candy—everything that accompanies dating. Eventually, "little boy" learns to appreciate the girl as a whole person.

While men are typically known as soul-modest, women are exactly the opposite. They are body-modest. Women tend to be guarded with their bodies. They pamper, care for, and preserve their bodies much more than men. A quick glance at "her bathroom" compared to "his bathroom" will confirm this tendency. To a guy, "skin care" often means nothing more than a bar of soap and some shaving cream. Female skin care has spawned a veritable pocket dictionary: moisturizers, clarifiers, exfoliates, hydrators, enhancers, buffers, etc. Yet for all of this physical pampering and modesty, women are not typically soul-modest.

Any given Sunday, after delivering my sermon I'll post myself in the lobby of whatever church I happen to be visiting. Men and women approach me to offer feedback, give suggestions, or ask further questions. Sometimes they will even share personal experiences that relate to my sermon. In all of my years on the road, I have never heard a man bare his soul in a church lobby. However, I have encountered numerous women who just opened the floodgates. In the span of a few short seconds, she can divulge every dark family secret while her husband stands by, visibly flinching at her honesty. I can almost hear his thoughts, *Dear God, woman, don't tell him that!*

You see, contrary to most men, women are very honest about themselves. There seems to be very little middle ground when it comes to women. In the pages of the Bible you tend to see women who are either the very best or the very worst, period. You see the Marys, the Hannahs, and the Elizabeths, or you see the Jezebels. One reason for consistent honesty, whether good or evil, is the female heart. Women are sure of their heart. In contrast, men know their abilities much more than they know their heart. Ladies can be incredibly honest because their heart is firm, it is sure, and it is certain. The female heart is the source, the very wellspring of life.

The struggle often comes when women try to share their heart with others. Men know how to be honest and accurate, they just choose not to be. With women it's different. Women choose to be honest about their heart but honesty is often frustrated by communication. Ladies, sometimes you must feel like you're speaking a foreign language. Men just don't seem to understand. The communication gap is so profound, so enduring that we've construed a planetary difference—the ol' Mars and Venus debate. Ladies, what seems very clear to you will generate responses like, "Ah, c'mon, mom, lighten up," or, "That's just the little woman talking again." You'd like to snap back, "Well, the 'little woman' has been right fifteen times in a row, you turkey," but you suspect that would just injure his poor little ego. It can be so frustrating when you understand your heart, when you are so honest with yourself and with others, but they don't seem to get it.

Before a couple gets married the man probably finds his thoughts drifting to the physical relationship (big surprise). It's not that women don't think about sex, they just tend to frame it in more romantic terms—the passion that comes from sharing. A woman will probably find herself enchanted with thoughts of pillow talk. You know, having a special person to share her thoughts, concerns, fears, and goals. This sharing not only accompanies physical intimacy, but actually surpasses it in some ways, truly cleaving and weaving two lives together. Two or three weeks after the wedding she finds herself cuddled up next to her new hubby. She's sharing her heart and after about ten minutes he finally responds… with a piercing snore. That's the first revelation, isn't it ladies? It's sort of all downhill after that. You wonder how he can be so dense at times. Why doesn't he recognize what you are trying to share? Why is it so hard to communicate your understanding and your vision? Sometimes, men just don't get it.

This pattern can produce an emotion called jealousy in the heart of a woman. It's not so much jealousy that someone else's husband looks like Tom Selleck, or that they have buckets of money. Those things aren't necessarily bad but this jealousy sounds more like, "Why am I not appreciated? Why am I not understood?" It becomes so frustrating. You want so badly to be understood, for your heart to be valued. When you aren't understood, when you aren't valued, the pain cuts like a knife. It cuts at the very center of your being. You consistently extend yourself and you are consistently unappreciated. Sometimes it seems like you work a full-time job outside the home and another full-time job inside the home, yet no one seems to recognize how much it costs or what it requires. You wish so much that someone (anyone!) would just appreciate you. I warn you ladies, if you allow jealousy to take root you will lose vision. You will lose vision for your husband and you will lose vision for your family. You will lose vision for everything that God has called you to be and to accomplish.

Shortly after our wedding, my wife and I invited my family over for our first big dinner. I'll be honest - I was absolutely clueless about the social undertones. Elaine was not. This was not only the first meal with her in-laws, but my father was also pastor of our church. Along with my mother and sister, Elaine was hosting her father-in-law and her pastor. It was a big deal. As dinner hosts we didn't have a full set of anything, but we did have a few parts: parts of china and parts of crystal. We also had a round table with four chairs and a stool. In true newlywed fashion, we lived in an apartment about the size of a Volkswagen.

Elaine said, "When your folks arrive, why don't we immediately sit at the table. We can pray, I'll sit on the stool, and they can sit on the chairs. I'll go into the kitchen to prepare your parents' plates. I'll serve them, then I'll go back and make you and your sister's plates. I'll serve you guys, then I'll go back and make my own plate. I'll come back and we can all eat together." I thought, *Good idea.*

The evening started as planned. After my folks were seated Elaine said, "Why don't we pray." We prayed, and then Elaine served my parents. She said, "Go ahead and eat, don't wait for me." Big mistake. That's when everything fell apart. Remember, I came from a pastor's home. I am convinced that pastors are some of the fastest eaters on the face of the earth. It all has to do with the telephone. It's almost like one of those natural laws we mentioned earlier. It goes something like this: every time a pastor sits down to eat, the telephone rings. It changes your entire approach to dining. Things become very simple. You try to beat the phone. You learn to eat at warp speed—*sluuurp*—"Ah, we won!" That was my family background. In contrast, Elaine came from a family that chewed everything repeatedly and for long periods of time. To say they didn't rush through a meal is an understatement. Her suggestion to my folks was an altogether innocent and polite gesture. She had no idea that she had unleashed the hounds. She made the same mistake when serving my sister and me, "Go ahead and eat." By the time Elaine prepared her own plate and sat down, we were all done.

Now, I'd only moved out of my folks' home three weeks earlier. We didn't have a whole lot to talk about. The only thing on my mind was something you can't talk about with your folks. I mean how do you say, "Dad, sex is good. It really is." So it was sort of quiet around the table. Elaine was there eating...and chewing...very slowly. We were all just staring at her. Finally she said, "Let's go sit on the sofa and talk for a while." We did. Eventually my family left.

They were no sooner out the door when—

"I'm not inviting your folks for dinner anymore!"

"Why not?!"

"They didn't appreciate it."

"How do you know?"

"They just inhaled it."

"But it was good!"

"How do you know? It didn't even touch your tongue!"

Believe it or not, I had no idea what she was talking about. Moreover, this wasn't a one-time event. Our sons inherited the pastor's eating legacy (maybe the generational sin of the culinary world). As you might imagine, the trait was magnified during football season. Sunday dinner became a race to catch the second-half of the game. Thanksgiving got downright dangerous. One year I remember Elaine saying, "You know what I'm going to do? So as not to slow you guys down, I think I'll just puree this meal so you can suck it up with a straw."

Some of you ladies know that feeling don't you? They never seem to appreciate it. "Ma, that was good—*belch*," and off they go! If you try to talk about it they say, "What do you mean?" No matter how articulate you happen to be, no matter how well-versed in the arts of rhetoric or persuasion, sometimes you feel utterly helpless to communicate. Here's the rub: if it only boiled down to sloppy eating habits you could probably live with the situation, but it doesn't. When vital needs and serious situations come to the surface you can feel utterly forsaken. More than unsupported, more than unappreciated, you are altogether invisible—maddening! It seems the very heavens have abandoned you.

One of the most surprising and utterly tragic things I have witnessed during more than two decades of travel is the rampant nature of abuse within the church. Abuse is not just out there in the world. It is also in the church. After talking with scores of individuals, pastors, counselors, and church staff, I believe it—totally.

Abuse is the gift that keeps on giving. It is utterly destructive, undermining everything from self-worth to trust in God. As a child she probably thinks, "Daddy had to do this to me, I wasn't a very good girl." As a wife she might say, "If I could just be a better spouse, my husband wouldn't do this to me." Then one day she wakes up and realizes, "I was not a bad daughter, I was not a bad wife. Daddy and my husband were bad men." In the resulting rage she screams, "God! Where were you?! Why didn't you protect me?!" When she sees other women apparently sailing through life without a care, it feels like a divine slap in the face. Anger compounds with jealousy. "Why me?! Why did I have to suffer this?"

The pattern is no mistake, the outcome is not unintended, and the cycle is not new. You may have heard the ol' phrase, "Those who ignore history are bound to repeat it." Unfortunately, our churches have demonstrated a profound historical ignorance. We cannot fall into the trap of thinking that we are sufficiently enlightened to ignore history. Unhistorical people are not enlightened, they are suckers. Anyone who fails to heed history is set-up for the Deceiver's same old lie. I challenge you ladies to recognize what is happening in the cycle of abuse. It represents a focused attack on our culture and on our churches. Here is a critical historical truth: every great revival in Church history can be traced to the united prayer of believers. Women are vitally important to this endeavor. Just as a man's outward orientation produces razor sharp evaluative abilities, a woman's inward orientation creates powerful intercessory capacities.

What do you think happens to a culture when Satan convinces women that their bodies are private temples to use any way they please (contra 1Cor. 6:19)? What happens when they end up angry, bitter, and frustrated after three or four abortions? The anger and jealousy are absolutely consuming. Not only that, after any number of sexual partners they feel almost no bond with their current husband. When they turn to the professional world they find themselves bumping up against glass ceilings, sexual harassment, and a culture that says, "Flaunt it if you've got it, baby. Don't worry about the consequences."

Do you think those kind of situations engender the intercessory prayer of women? I think not. Do you think that women who find themselves abused and unappreciated at church are going to have a vision for their family? For their community? I think not. The issue is very simple. Ladies, your insight and awareness, your deep spiritual understanding creates a profound ability to intercede and to change your world. But, if jealousy takes center stage, intercession will never happen. Rage will supplant vision.

I really appreciate the book of Ruth. However, I believe the book is misnamed. I think it should be called the book of Naomi. I know it's a nice love story, I know Ruth is the cute young thing, and I know Naomi doesn't have the flashiest role. If this book was a movie, Doris Day would play Ruth, Ronald Reagan would play Boaz, and the part of Naomi would probably go to Angela Lansbury. Marketing considerations aside, notice how the story unfolds. Notice how Naomi plays a central role. Also, keep in mind the historical setting. We can tell this tale in modern language, but we dare not strip away cultural context. Naomi had no concept of modern (let alone postmodern) Western culture. Before Enlightenment attitudes, Naomi lived and breathed in the context of rigorous social law.

One day, Naomi's husband comes to her and drops a bombshell. "Wife, we have to move to the land of the Moabites because of this famine." Our first thought would probably be something like, "Ugh, what a pain in the neck— boxes, packing tape, styrofoam pellets, dollies, and trucks. Yuck." Surely Naomi's move had inconveniences, but the repercussions of this bombshell went a whole lot deeper than the hassles of transplanting a family nest. Ladies, you need to understand what it would have meant to a woman of Judah. It was horrific. First of all, the greatest anointing, blessing, and vision for a Jewish woman was to bear a male child. You can label this whatever you'd like. You can call it chauvinistic or you can call it petty, but that's the way it was. Second to having a male child was seeing that child marry into the lineage of Abraham, Isaac, and Jacob. That was Naomi's cultural framework and that was her calling. That's what she knew. It would have been her driving passion from childhood. Given that context, imagine all of a sudden having to pack-up and move the two (unmarried!) boys to Moab.

Moab wasn't just the wrong side of the tracks. It was the wrong side of the planet. It was an utterly ungodly place. Do you remember when God told Abraham to leave Ur of the Chaldeans to spend the rest of his life traveling and living in a tent (Gen. 12:1)? Do you remember that wherever his foot trod was promised as an inheritance (Gen. 12:7)? Do you remember his nephew, named Lot (Gen. 12:4)? After several years of wandering Lot came to his uncle and said, "Uncle, you know it's really crowded up here in the hills and my air mattress keeps going flat on all these rocks. I would really like to go down to the valley where our sheep will have a little more to eat, where the land isn't so rough, and where my air mattress won't take such a beating." Uncle Abe says, "Wait a second. Those valley folk are trouble. Don't get too close to Sodom and Gomorrah." Lot replies, "Oh, no, no. We'll just get close enough so we can watch cable TV and the kids can ride the bus to school. We won't get any closer than that." Well, they got so close that when angelic messengers came to rescue Lot and his family, he was willing to throw his daughters to a mob who wanted to rape the visiting messengers (Gen. 19:8). That's how close he got. Lot's wife was so enmeshed that she couldn't bear to leave without one last glimpse. What's the trouble with one last glimpse? She became a pillar of salt, that's what. Lot and his two daughters were left seeking shelter in a cave.

Male children were just as important to Lot's girls as they would have been to Naomi. The daughters decide not to let any moss grow under their feet. They say, "If we don't do something quickly, our posterity will end." Trouble. What's the solution? Break out the booze, get their father drunk, and have an incestuous relationship (Gen. 19:32). The resulting lineage was the tribe of Moab. As if incestuous origins weren't bad enough, the Israelites also detested Moab because her citizens actively opposed Israel during the wilderness wanderings (Num. 22:4-6). Not only that, Moab was one of the nations that invited Israel to offer sacrifices to false gods (Num. 25:1-3), even to the point of offering children as human sacrifices. Can you imagine your husband coming and saying, "Wife, we have to move to a place that is absolutely ungodly and demonic. They were birthed in incest and they sacrifice children by passing them through fire." Your reply would be something like, "NO!" And then I'm sure Naomi said, "But husband, our two boys are about to start dating. They won't find any good Jewish girls. All those valley girls wear lots of make-up and real short skirts. Our boys will be sitting ducks." Husband probably replied, "Well, if we stay here they're gonna starve to death. What do you want to do? Do you want them to die or should we go to Moab?" Not much of a choice, huh, ladies?

They travel to Moab and Naomi's husband dies. Isn't that the way it always goes, ladies? The guy who got you into this mess bails out! Can you believe it? He dies on her. I know I said that guys are great at withdrawing, but this is ridiculous. Naomi was left in a foreign land with two sitting duck sons. What happened? First one, then the other: Moabite daughter-in-laws. She knew it. For ten years they remained in the land of Moab.

That brings us to verse five of the first chapter of the book of Naomi (Ruth). "Then both [of her sons] also died, and the woman was bereft of her two children and her husband." Bereft, ripped away, torn from her side, void, empty, gone. Can you imagine the pain, ladies? She was empty. She was totally and completely bereft. Nothing was left. Her two boys, her vision and her pride, were first given to the "wrong girls" and then completely ripped away. Think about this: why did they have to go to Moab in the first place? Because of a famine. What is a famine? It's an act of God. Why did God do this to her? Why did God allow conditions that forced her husband to move south?

Ladies, just like you, Naomi could have looked around and seen other women who were protected from problems. Just like you, she could have seen other ladies who seemed to skip through life with a pretty little smile. Sometimes you just want to slap 'em, don't you? They're just always so happy. "Why do you have to smile so much?!" Of course, you're trying to be happy too but it just ticks you off! They don't ever seem to have the same kind of struggles. Why didn't God save Naomi? I often wonder if Naomi didn't have a sister back in the land of Judah whose husband was some sort of CPA. He was probably making big bucks and both of their kids were doing just swell. Maybe Naomi got word from Judah every so often, "It's wonderful up here. How's everything down there?" Ladies, sometimes jealousy and anger can be directed towards God, can't they? You can be jealous of the way He seems to treat others.

So here's Naomi with two Moabite daughter-in-laws. She's bereft of her husband and sons. She has nothing left. She turns to the girls and says, "I'm going back to Judea. Girls, you return to your fathers and find new husbands because even if I had a son in my womb tonight it would be twenty years before he was any good to either of you." She knew the vision but she also saw the circumstances. Again, we have to be aware of the cultural context. Her strongest message to the girls may be somewhat lost on us. We might just think, "Well, you know, she was kind." It's more than that. We have to recognize the social context. In Naomi's culture, Social Security and Medicare hadn't kicked in. Society was built around family. Naomi had two daughters-in-law and they were her support. If she released these girls, she was releasing the very means of her support and security. She could very well starve. The two daughters-in-law know this and offer culturally expected objections, "Oh no, mom! We couldn't do it. No, no, no." Naomi is firm, "I mean it, girls, go." Naomi starts walking away. She turns around, "Now, girls, I really mean it, go home." She keeps walking. Finally one girl turns back.

I imagine the next scene happening at sunset near the top of a mountain. The birds are chirping and Julie Andrews is in the background singing "Climb Every Mountain." It's a romantic song, ladies—it's been sung at countless weddings. Naomi turns around and says, "Ruth, girl, what are you doing?" Ruth's answer is the stuff of legends, "Do not urge me to leave you or turn back from following you; for where you go, I will go, and where you lodge, I will lodge. Your people shall be my people, and your God, my God. Where you die, I will die, and there I will be buried. Thus may the LORD do to me, and worse, if anything but death parts you and me," (Ruth 1:16-17). Whoa! Again, understand what was happening. In our terminology, Ruth the Moabitess just got "saved." She just committed herself to the lordship of Yahweh. She just promised anything and everything she could ever be or have: wherever you go, whoever your people, wherever you die, whoever your God—shall be to me as well.

Where could a girl from a pagan, ungodly culture have learned such faith? There were no Gideon Bibles, no motivational cassettes, no Christian churches, no seminars or books, and no Christian TV or radio—none of it! There was only one source for this Moabite girl to witness saving faith: Naomi. She witnessed faith from the same woman who could have been a source of uncontrollable rage and jealousy. Naomi could have been the worst, shrewish nightmare of a mother-in-law you ever heard of. She was bereft! Her husband bailed out on her, her sons died, her sister back in Judea was writing all these stupid letters, and she ended up with two Moabite daughters-in-law. If anyone had a right to be ticked off, Naomi did. Yet Ruth obviously observed a powerful love and a saving faith. If Naomi had been the mother-in-law from hell and she had said, "Girls, go home—," *pshoong*, those girls would have been making tracks at the speed of light. Do you see the point? Ladies, when everything seems to fall apart, a faithful heart can produce the fulfillment of your vision. You can be the intercessor, the one who literally changes history. But, if jealousy rages and if anger is directed at God, you may never see your vision realized.

When the widows get back to Judea they have two options. They can starve to death, or they can glean. A gleaner was little more than a scavenger—a socially acceptable scavenger, but a scavenger nonetheless. Gleaning was a legal provision that allowed poor folk to rummage a farmer's field during harvest. The law commanded farmers to stop reaping short of the very corners of their field (Lev. 19:9-10). Moreover, if a harvester forgot about one sheaf and started working on another, he couldn't go back to pick up the first one (Deut. 24:19). Forgotten sheaves were the lot of gleaners—the poor, the alien, the fatherless, and the widow. If you had any dignity, gleaning wasn't a whole lot better than starving.

Imagine how farmers would have resisted the gleaning proviso. First, think about the economics involved. Jewish farmers would surely have learned to reap within about three or four centimeters of the very corner. "We'll abide by the law, just barely." You don't think so? Ancient Jewish culture was worlds apart from modern Western culture, but the human heart was just as sinful, just as selfish. God's law recognized this from the start. The command: "there will be no poor among you," (Deut. 15:4). The reality: "the poor will never cease to be in the land," (Deut. 15:11). The command: "do not be hardhearted or tightfisted toward your poor brother...give generously to him and do so without a grudging heart," (Deut. 15:7,10—NIV). The reality: take a wild guess. I'm not ignoring the culture. Gleaners faced slim-pickings and if a farmer had a fumble-fingered harvester, he probably became a gleaner the next day. In addition to economics, there were surely strong social dimensions. Do you think these farmers wanted all the "poor trash" to come stomping down their tulips and gathering their stuff? It had to be worse than Spring Break in Florida. "Get out of here! Get off my property!" Gleaning was part of God's provision, part of His very structure for ancient Israel, but it wasn't pleasant for either party involved.

How do you think Ruth felt that first morning when she sat up in bed, pulled on her Levi's, strapped on some work boots, and headed out the door? "Me and my big mouth! All of that *your people, my people* stuff. I'm going gleaning!" Not only that, these were the days of the judges (Ruth 1:1). In case you don't know, the period of the judges was not the heyday of Israelite morality (Jdg. 2:10-19). The moral climate could easily give rise to another concern. "I'm a foreign woman, in a foreign land, in a field full of men. I'm a sitting duck to get raped." Furthermore, just to dispel any other romantic ideas you might be entertaining, realize that Ruth had no thermos, no lunchbox, and nothing even close to a porta-potty. Things didn't look very bright. "Even if I do get a little grain, somebody will probably whack me on the head, steal my grain, and I'll have worked all day for nothing." These were all legitimate concerns, but notice what happens.

As Ruth is gleaning that morning, the owner of the property arrives. It just so happens that she's found herself in the field of a man named Boaz. We don't know what Boaz looked like, and the hints we do have suggest there were more attractive guys on the market (Ruth 3:10), but that doesn't matter. In this story, good ol' Boaz plays the knight in shining armor. He couldn't have looked any better if he had come swooping in on a big white horse with Tom Selleck's dimple on his chin and everything. In Ruth's eyes he must have looked absolutely wonderful. Here's why. He jumps off his horse and says to the foreman, "Who's the young woman?" The foreman replies, "That's the Moabitess who came back with your close relative." "Oh, she's the one. Listen to me, foreman, you tell these men that if anyone lays a finger on that woman they'll deal with me. She's been good to my close relative. What is more, foreman, when it's lunchtime you let her feed herself and refresh herself with my maidens in my home. When the day is over, you let her go into my home to refresh herself, you give her a bag of grain, and you see that she gets home safely." Not bad.

You can just imagine around sunset as Ruth comes dragging this huge load of grain into the house and Naomi goes, "Whoa, girl! Where did you get a bag like that?!" "Oh mom, I went to some field and in the middle of the morning this wonderful guy (he was better than Tom Selleck, mom), he drives up on his big white horse and he says to the foreman, 'don't touch her' and all the rest of that. It was wonderful, mom!"

The two widows not only survive but thrive. After what must have been a record-setting season for any gleaner, Naomi has a little chat with Ruth. "You know what, girl?" "What?" "Tonight Boaz is going to be winnowing barley. When it gets late I want you to take a shower, perfume yourself, put on your cutest dress, get your blanket, and go lay down next to him on the threshing floor." Ruth's heart goes, *thump*! "What?! This is a weird country, mom. I know I said 'wherever' and 'whatever' but this is weird."

Let's take a reality check. You might be thinking this is completely chauvinistic, as if Ruth is just a piece of meat, but ladies I want you to know that God never treats you with anything less than full respect. Nothing in world history has been better for womankind than the legacy of Yahweh and the Lordship of Jesus Christ. If you don't believe me, look at some pagan religions of the past. Womankind is blessed because of Jesus Christ. This is not "piece of meat" theology, this is called posterity. This is about God's covenant, the blessing of all humanity through Abraham's offspring (Gen. 12:2-3). God has endowed women with a powerful maternal instinct. Even in our individualized, privatized, highly modern and consumer-driven society, even in a culture where traditional family roles have become optional rather than expected, inconvenient rather than blessed, even today the so-called biological clock is a powerful force. If Murphy Brown's biological clock can turn her world upside down, imagine what it could do in a culture where a woman's highest calling was to bear male children. Imagine what it could do if a woman's husband died and there was no provision for her to fulfill that calling. That's what this is all about.

Ruth goes to the threshing floor, rolls out her blanket, and lays down next to Boaz. He rolls over and wakes up.

"Who's there?"

"Ruth, the Moabitess—the one in the field."

"Oh, my close relative's daughter-in-law."

"Yes."

"Ruth, I recognize why you are here. You have demonstrated incredible loyalty, incredible love. Do you understand how the law has established the raising up of posterity?"

"Yeah."

"The point is, Ruth, it's the closest kin. I am your kin, but there is a closer relative."

Right about now you can imagine Ruth thinking, *Oh, dear God!* Ladies, you understand this feeling, don't you? You've been to the proverbial threshing floor. It's like you just start trusting God and you get another curve thrown at you.

"A 'closer'?"

"That's right, Ruth. I tell you what, I'll take care of it. I want you to leave before sunrise so your character won't be disparaged, and I want you to take more grain when you leave."

Again, imagine sunrise as Ruth drags home even more grain and Naomi goes, "What happened?!"

"Nothing!"

"What do you mean, nothing?!"

"There's a 'closer' still around."

"Oh my, I'm sorry, girl. Well, what did Boaz say?"

"He said, 'trust me.'"

Ha! Don't you love that one, ladies? "Trust me." Yeah, right. But the point is that if you can't trust, the alternatives are suspicion, anger, fear, and jealousy. You have to trust. Look at everything God has done to demonstrate His trustworthiness. At this point it's up to Ruth to exercise faith and step into the gap. Faith is demonstrated in critical moments. Ruth has reached the point of critical decision. This is where Ruth realizes what she committed herself to. Much more than a spiffy song about "wherever you go, I will go," this is the real thing.

Meanwhile, Boaz goes to the city gate and sits with the elders. After a while the closer relative finally shuffles by. Boaz says, "Friend, come here and sit with me. You know the piece of land that belonged to Elimelech? Well, Naomi has returned from Moab and she wants to sell it. Do you think you want to farm that land?" Closer relative says, "Yep, I'm gonna keep it." That's when Boaz drops the other shoe (or, the other sandal in this case). "By the way, the daughter-in-law came back with no kids." Woooo, that's all it takes. Suddenly, the closer relative doesn't want to touch this deal. He has no desire to dilute his estate and he's had it with diapers. He says, "Alright then, it's all yours." They exchange sandals (i.e., close escrow), and the deal is done.

That brings us to the fourth chapter and the thirteenth verse of the book of Naomi (Ruth). "So Boaz took Ruth, and she became his wife, and Boaz went in to her. And the LORD enabled her to conceive, and she gave birth to a son."

Amazing. From bereft in chapter one, to a grandson in chapter four. Ladies, what do you think would have happened if Naomi had exchanged faithfulness for anger? Sure, God is bigger than human sin but He longs to work through our faithfulness, He desires faithful obedience (1Sam. 15:22). What a joy to see Him work through you, not in spite of you. Notice what happened. Naomi didn't just put on a happy face and pretend that everything was okay. She felt genuinely abandoned by God, even felt God had dealt bitterly with her (Ruth 1:20-21). She wasn't immune to pain but she let the pain work in her. If she had allowed rage, jealousy, or anger to consume her, the vision might never have been fulfilled. But now, in verse fourteen of chapter four, "The women said to Naomi, 'Blessed is the LORD, who has not left you without a redeemer today, and may his name become famous in Israel,'" (Ruth 4:14).

A redeemer! Ladies, you might feel like you're always left twisting in the wind. Maybe you feel like you always end up with the fuzzy end of the lollipop. Maybe you just have no one left to trust. I want you to know, God has not left you without a redeemer. Naomi goes from bereft to redeemed. Notice what else the neighbor women say, "May he also be to you a restorer of life and a sustainer of your old age; for your daughter-in-law, who loves you and is better to you than seven sons, has given birth to him," (Ruth 4:15b). What a powerful testimony! These are the same neighbors who could have been wagging and clucking their tongues at the angry widow and the dirty Moabitess. But, Naomi's faith bore fruit in the life of Ruth. When this young pagan was redeemed, she embodied Israel's great call—to be a source of blessing to all nations (Gen. 12:3). Though God's law often degenerated into legalism, it was intended as a tool of wisdom and instruction. Naomi was faithful to the call, and God supplied a redeemer in her old age. Ruth was better than seven sons—the full quiver, the full provision, the whole enchilada, baby.

"The neighbor women gave him a name, saying, 'A son has been born to Naomi!' So they named him Obed. He is the father of Jesse, the father of David," (Ruth 4:17). By the way, that's King David. A pagan girl becomes the great-grandmother of a king and a bereft widow becomes the great, great-grandmother of a king. Not only that, twenty-eight generations after King David, the King of Kings hangs on a cross with Moabite blood in His lineage. The ultimate gift "to whosoever" includes the story of a woman who didn't lose vision in the face of incredible jealousy, bitterness, and anger.

In 1984 our thirteen-year-old daughter, Julie, died from congenital heart disease. When Julie died, my wife Elaine was left with a very male household:

a male husband, two male sons, a male dog, a male cat, a male bird, and we think a male fish (I wasn't going to check). Needless to say, the place was dripping with testosterone. Elaine's only daughter, her greatest source of empathy and understanding, had been taken. She was bereft. Julie had just reached adolescence so she and Elaine were starting to reach a whole new level of intimacy. They started wearing some of the same clothes, they stood around discussing PMS, and they'd go to stores that smelled like dead weeds (potpourri). Suddenly, Elaine was alone in a male cauldron. She was never angry or disappointed with her sons but the grief was overwhelming. All of the mother-daughter relationships she saw around her felt like a divine slap in the face. It didn't matter whether other relationships were bumpy or smooth, weak or strong. Whatever those relationships looked like, at least there was something. Elaine was bereft.

The jealousy, the anger, and the depression could have destroyed our two sons, especially our oldest. Greg was fifteen years old when Julie died. He was a sophomore in high school. Despite his youth, Greg was quite a traveler. You see, all of my trekking and speaking meant that Greg had attended eight schools by the time he was in the eighth grade. He had been through about six or eight reading systems and he was a tad confused. He was struggling, not for any learning disabilities but because he was confused. Due to Greg's academic record, Elaine was invited to the counselor's office. Consistent with an unfortunate legacy of liberal mediocrity, the counselors encouraged Elaine to lower her sights. "Never expect more than C's, because that's all Greg can do. Also, never talk about sending him to college." Ooooh, that was a red flag for momma. She worked, she invested, and Greg began to turn the corner. He graduated from high school with close to a B-average. He spent one semester at a small Christian school, and then transferred to a community college. His big break came in the form of an English professor whose son had traveled a similar path. This professor knew how to speak Greg's language, and things finally clicked. Next stop: college. Greg had proved those counselors wrong.

The right combination of divine timing and provision sent Greg to a great university. It was a dream for him to attend, and a dream for us to send him. In the middle of Greg's sophomore year, Elaine and I happened to visit a couple of dear friends. We had known this husband and wife for years. In fact, I had worked at the same church with the husband twenty years earlier. In the course of our visit, they started asking about Greg's school. It turned out that their daughter wanted to transfer schools and Greg's school sounded like just the right place. At the start of Greg's junior year (which happened to be her junior year as well), she transferred.

It's pretty easy for parents to put one and one together and come up with two. I mean, hey, old friends and everything. At the same time, we knew if we said anything it would be the kiss of death. "Hey Greg, have you thought about dating this girl?" "Never!" For some reason, parental dating advice was about as appealing as dog lips. So, we held our tongues. We'd make allusions, he'd laugh.

Everything changed at the beginning of their senior year when the school hosted a fall social. This was a Quaker college so school-sponsored parties were few-and-far-between. You just didn't let something like this pass you by. Besides, Greg's roommate bet him that he couldn't get a date. That well-placed bet was just the right incentive for a man known to say, "I'd rather spend money on myself." After attending the fall social Greg and the family friend weren't officially dating, but they were suddenly spending a lot of time together. Elaine and I were quite pleasantly dumbstruck.

After our daughter died, the first Christmas was simply hell. Julie was born December 1st, so Christmas was her private fiefdom. The first holiday without her was just horrible. Elaine said, "We need to do something about this," so we started a new family tradition. Fortunately, my work affords plenty of free time during the holidays. For some reason churches would rather schedule Christmas parties and Christmas cantatas than itinerant preachers. Elaine said, "Since you can't get meetings why don't we learn to ski and take the boys up to a lodge?" I was forty-one years old, and hadn't skied since I was seventeen. Elaine had skied only once in her entire life. Despite these rather significant obstacles, we resolved to make this a family venture. We weren't going to just ship the boys off by themselves. So, shortly after Elaine's brainstorm we found ourselves standing on a couple of slick rails and facing a sheet of ice with absolutely no brake pedals—brilliant. Thankfully, we not only survived many years on the slopes, we actually learned a thing or two. It was incredible.

Since we had established this family tradition years before Greg met the family friend, it was a perfectly pregnant opportunity (no pun intended). We said, "Greg, why don't you invite this young lady so we can get to know her?" He invited, and she came. As we were lounging in the lodge one evening, Greg and this young lady were walking a few feet in front of Elaine and I. She slid her arm through Greg's arm and they started walking down the corridor butting hips. I poked Elaine, leaned over and said, "It's all over." Momma wasn't completely certain, but I was.

They graduated in May of 1992. It was a terrible year for college-level entry positions. Greg couldn't find any work in our area, and the young woman decided to move back to Indianapolis to be close to her parents (who had since relocated). Odd as it may seem, Greg developed a deep burden for the Midwest. I said, "If you move back there, Greg, do you know what it will mean?" He said, "I know." They were officially engaged in September of 1992. On August 7, 1993 her father and I officiated our two children's wedding. It was a special moment.

The reason I've recounted this little love tale is that at the close of the ceremony I turned to my son and said, "Greg, do you take this woman, Julie, to be your lawfully wedded wife?" God gave us back a Julie. It wasn't the same. In fact, it was actually an obstacle when they first met. It was about three dates into their relationship before Greg could even call her by name. Here's the point. It wasn't supposed to be the same and there are absolutely no guarantees for the future. The point is not about specific outcomes. The point is about God's faithful character. We had the privilege of witnessing God's redemption. We had lost our daughter, we were bereft, and there was nothing we could do. God gave us back a Julie, a Julie brought into our family by love. I absolutely commend and honor my wife. If she had lost the vision, if she had let herself be consumed by jealousy, anger, or depression, Greg might never have made it to college. We might never have witnessed God's restoration and redemption in the form of another Julie. Ladies, don't lose the vision.

4

ENDURANCE IN MEN:
A MATTER OF ACTION

Then the men of Israel said to Gideon, "Rule over us, both you and your son, also your son's son, for you have delivered us from the hand of Midian." But Gideon said to them, "I will not rule over you, nor shall my son rule over you; the LORD shall rule over you." Yet Gideon said to them, "I would request of you, that each of you give me an earring from his spoil."

~ Judges 8:22-24a

My wife and I recently had the privilege of traveling to Rome. In the midst of various ministry responsibilities, we had a few hours to visit the ancient ruins. If you have ever visited the Coliseum or the Forum Romana, you understand the sheer awe of touching the foundations of Western civilization. How many places have 2,000 year-old buildings, let alone 2,000 year-old street dust? Not my neighborhood.

Behind the Roman Senate, the building from which the power of Rome flowed, the building from whose steps Augustus proclaimed taxes on the entire world, behind the grandeur and majesty was a tiny spot. It was a hole, literally, it was a hole. The spot was once part of an open road but now a church surrounds, shelters, and houses it. The hole remains. More importantly, the dungeon beneath the hole remains. To accommodate tourists, a stairwell—a bypass if you will—provides access to the dungeon. This bypass circumvents the need to be lowered by a rope. Like any good dungeon, this subterranean prison is dark, damp, and small.

As I descended the steps, the first thing I noticed was my head brushing against the ceiling. Next, I noticed that a few lights had been installed. Rather than dressing-up the place, they merely highlighted the fact that this was a little corner of hell hewn out of lava. In its heyday, the dungeon was conveniently stationed above a river of sewage. In this place, near the river of Roman sewage, a round iron loop was fastened to the wall. In the middle of this loop was an iron peg. From this peg, prisoners were manacled and chained, strung-up above a river of sewage. When the prisoner's life was spent the sewer provided a convenient means of disposal.

The name of this dungeon is "Paul's Prison." There's no way to know for sure, but this prison very possibly housed the Apostle Paul (if it wasn't this specific prison, it was probably one very similar). More than any of the grandeur or majesty of Imperial Rome, I was overwhelmed by the dismal dungeon that held Paul. I simply stood in that prison with tears in my eyes thinking, *Dear God...*How often we, as men and women of the church, grumble. How often we feel inconvenienced, troubled, or just plain bored. How often we feel as if we deserve something better. Our father in the faith was banished to a hole.

This same man wrote a letter to the Roman church before visiting their congregation(s). Ironically, Paul's letter expressed his great desire to come and to minister in their city, not knowing his wish would be granted in the form of chains and bonds. Paul's letter also spoke powerfully of God's providence in the midst of suffering, "And we know that God causes all things to work together for good to those who love God, to those who are called according to His purpose... Who will separate us from the love of Christ? Will tribulation, or distress, or persecution, or famine, or nakedness, or peril, or sword?" (Rom. 8:28,35). No, none of these things will separate us from Christ's love—nothing will, nothing can (Rom. 8:38,39).

I stood in that dungeon wondering, *Did those words come back to Paul?* More importantly, *Did those words come back to haunt Paul?* If you look at the second letter that Paul wrote to Timothy, his adopted son in the Lord, you get a clear picture of his heart and mind as he neared life's end. "For I am already being poured out as a drink offering, and the time of my departure has come. I have fought the good fight, I have finished the course, I have kept the faith," (2Tim. 4:6-7). There was no sense of conflict, no sense of doubt or being haunted by his earlier words. Paul stood firm and strong. However, he was fully human. Immediately following his declaration of strength he says, "Come quickly, Timothy." We detect no whining and no self-pity, but we do detect Paul's humanity. "Come quickly, Timothy, for I have sent some to their responsibilities and others have deserted me. Only Luke is left. Bring my cloak. Stop by and pick up those books and parchments—especially the parchments... come quickly, Timothy." We glimpse the man facing humanity at the brink of death.

Paul's prison was quite a different picture from modern Western prisons. As I have already indicated, Roman dungeons weren't equipped with conveniences. Forget about televisions and DVD's, these guys couldn't even play tic-tac-toe. Not only that, but Roman guards didn't furnish any sort of care or provision for their prisoners. There was no food, no water—nothing. If you were imprisoned and you had no friends, things were pretty bleak. With Paul's words to Timothy echoing in my mind, I stood in that dungeon imagining what it might have been like.

It's so easy to look at Paul's circumstances, even easier to look at our own circumstances, and think, "Can that be God? Can that be the work of a good and loving God?" Yet Paul, imprisoned in the shadow of Rome's great Coliseum, realized that the crown and the prize come to those who finish their course (2Tim. 4:8). The Coliseum was a place of gruesome carnage. It was also a place of vigorous competition. Athletes trained, competed, and disciplined themselves, even punishing their bodies (cf. 1Cor. 9:24-27), all for the dignity and honor bestowed by a grass crown. Evoking these strong and well-known images, Paul said, "I'm going to get my crown! I'm going to endure!"

Like so many others, I often struggle with endurance. As with vision, the battle for endurance is common to humanity. In fact, the two battles are intimately linked. We will never see our vision fulfilled if we are unwilling to fight the battles of others (i.e., to endure), or if we are unwilling to trust (i.e., to endure). As with vision, the battle lines for endurance are uniquely drawn for men and women. This chapter will focus on endurance in men, and the next will focus on endurance in women.

With men, who I have described as visually and externally oriented, the equation is pretty simple: accomplishments fuel stamina. But what happens when accomplishments and affirmation disappear? Worse yet, what if they never materialize in the first place? "Why should I put up with this situation? What's the point? Phooey on it!" For men, so many obstacles to godly character boil down to a single issue: withdrawal. The tendency to withdraw is the most powerful temptation facing the eye of man. This is the trap of pulling back, protecting the ego, and avoiding potential embarrassment or shame. However, if we pull back and if we withdraw, how can we possibly finish the race? How can we possibly win the crown that God so desperately wants to bestow? It's easy for men to convince themselves that truly great achievements require special gifts, special know-how, or special training. Our culture does a wonderful job reinforcing this perception. I bet your local community college or technical school runs radio spots promising a way out of that "dead end" job you've got. If you just complete their evenings and weekends program you can take a step up in the world. I'm not in the business of bashing education or training, but realize that the true path to success (i.e., godly character) is one of endurance. Sure, a vision for bigger bucks and bigger cars might lead you to a bigger job. However, a bigger job won't make you a better man. Your most important achievements in life require nothing more than endurance—including that evening degree at your community college. More than know-how or training, endurance is a matter of choice. It is a matter of patient continuance. I challenge you men to endure, to realize that endurance is the path to godly character and true success.

Sometime very soon, my wife and I will commence our 987th diet over the span of just a few years. Some of you know what I'm talking about. There's no secret to dieting, it's just, "Do it, baby." Consistent discipline is all it takes. But see, by about the third day that celery starts tasting like a big ol' weed. It possesses absolutely none of the allure of chocolate cake. Go figure. By day four, at precisely 12:01 a.m., you throw your hands up and say, "I don't need this!" Not only that, you actually find a way to congratulate yourself for your abrupt withdrawal. "I've been dieting for two or three meals. That's got to count for something. I've got a pretty good metabolism. Who knows, maybe I've already lost eighteen pounds!" Don't get me wrong, your physique isn't necessarily an indicator of spiritual maturity, but so many spiritual principles are reflected, learned, and perfected in the physical world. In both spheres, you need endurance.

I challenge you seasoned saints (myself included) to endure. I challenge you young people to endure. Young or old, endure in your responsibilities and endure in your opportunities. We live in a land of incredible opportunity. We have so much opportunity and affluence that we often lack the motivation to endure. "Do I really feel like studying? Do I really feel like sacrificing my time in front of the TV? Nah." I challenge you to endure. As I said before, it's not just about educational degrees, incomes, and jobs. I challenge you to endure for the sake of your contribution to the Kingdom. Endure in your responsibilities and endure in your opportunities. Allow God to create in you something of value, not for the sake of a big income, a big car, or a big house on the hill, but for the sake of His Kingdom. Endure.

I know some of you struggle in your marriages. Some of you think, "I don't need to put up with this anymore." Not only that, the world says you have a right to feel that way. The world says it's natural (even healthy!) to feel that way. The world often says, "You don't need to put up with antiquated social norms. You can find a way around those promises you made. Just do whatever feels good. Nobody's perfect." How deeply have these attitudes penetrated our culture? In just the past few years, attitudes like these have allowed our nation to redefine concepts of adultery and appropriate action in the highest office of the land. You start thinking, "Hey, if it's good enough for the guy at the top, then it's good enough for me." I say, no! Endure in your relationships because therein lies true value. There is no lasting value in chalking up another score. What a crass and entirely degrading concept. In contrast, what value is found in marriages that endure. What value there is between spouses who consistently choose to honor and cherish each other through the trials of life, growing old together and having children who bless them. Therein lies value, but it demands endurance. It only comes through commitment, "Come what may, I will live through this. I will endure."

I challenge you to endure in your responsibilities at church. Some people say, "All the church cares about these days is money. All they talk about is money." But see, you have an obligation to your church. If the church is your spiritual home and your spiritual body, you have an obligation to that home and to that body. You have an obligation to support it. You wouldn't dine at a fine restaurant and then say, "You know, they don't need my cash." You wouldn't say, "You know, other people are covering their bills. I'm sure there's enough money to go around."

What if you have a problem with your child? What if you have a problem in your marriage? What if you have a problem with your health? You probably call the Youth Pastor, or get counsel, or ask for prayer. Maybe you've had those very things happen and you walked away feeling like your church resembled a fast food joint more than a fine restaurant. That's not the point. As a good capitalist, you understand the principle. Besides, if you wish your church functioned more like a fine restaurant then maybe it's time you rolled up your sleeves and got to work. It's your church.

I've also heard this one, "I can't trust 'em. Churches misuse money." Well, you trust your pastor to address your very soul every Sunday you sit in that pew. If that doesn't seem like a big deal, maybe you ought to reevaluate who else you're trusting with the privilege of speaking to your soul. You trust your church to counsel your kids and to keep your marriage together, but you mean to tell me that you can't trust the church with your money? Where are you storing up treasure? "Well, you know God, He can take care of it." Be very careful with those thoughts. God has given you the responsibility to be His vessel. "But in the New Testament it's all about grace. You don't really have to tithe." I don't think so. In the New Testament it's all about Lordship. In the Old Testament, God only asked for ten percent. In the New Testament, He demands everything (e.g., Matt. 19:21). All you really do with ten percent is pay rent, acknowledging God's ownership and His Lordship. "Why do we have to do it that way?" Because it all belongs to God anyway.

I challenge you to endure in your commitments. God will bless you in ways that you may not even begin to understand. More importantly, He will mold you into a person of character. So many times when problems, issues, or various circumstances arise we wonder, "How can this be God? I don't understand. Does God really work like this?" If you want to get an idea of the way God can work, just take a look at the story of Gideon.

Gideon is first mentioned in the sixth chapter of the book of Judges. We find him threshing wheat in a winepress. I don't know a whole lot about farming but I've figured out that most people don't thresh wheat in a winepress. It's a little unorthodox to say the least. Just as surprising is the greeting Gideon receives while he's stationed at the bottom of this winepress: "Hail, valiant warrior!" Something doesn't quite fit.

Let's set the stage. Israel is being oppressed by the Midianites. Ancient oppressors were notorious for two things. First, they would remove weapons. Second, they would take food. The Midianites were so effective at this that the Israelites took to living in mountains and caves (Jdg. 6:2). The Midianites were such great oppressors that they were described as swarming locusts (Jdg. 6:5). This sweet little relationship between conqueror and conquered not only made the conqueror stronger, it also made the conquered weaker. If you don't have adequate food and you don't have adequate weapons, you aren't going to mount much of a threat. Hence, Gideon was threshing in a winepress. He was hiding from the Midianites and trying to eek out some food for his family. He was probably scared to death.

Suddenly he hears, "Hail, valiant warrior!" After scraping his jaw off the bottom of the winepress Gideon must have thought, "What is this guy talking about?" Was it from God? Yes. This altogether surprising greeting was delivered by the Angel of the LORD. Gideon wasn't addressed by some overly optimistic zealot. This wasn't a human message. It was divine. Gideon was addressed by the Angel of the living God. "Valiant warrior," was God's assessment. He was summoning and calling forth what could develop through faithful endurance.

"Hail, valiant warrior! I've got a job for you. I want you to defeat the Midianites. Raise up an army and go forth." Ha! Gideon was impressed, but he wasn't quite convinced. He's going to need some assurance so he becomes the first guy in history to put out a fleece. He literally lays out the wool of a lamb on his threshing floor and says, "God, if this is really you...I think I saw an angel but things are kind of fuzzy now, so if this is really you and you really want me to raise up an army to defeat the Midianites, then make the fleece wet and the ground dry." He wakes up the next morning and that's exactly the way it is (Jdg. 6:38). A little bolder, but still not convinced, he says, "God, please don't get upset but if this is really you, and you really want me to do this, then make the ground wet and the fleece dry"—an even greater feat. Needless to say, he really wants to know that God is on his side. We know that feeling, don't we? "Is this God? Can this possibly be God?" Once again, God graciously grants assurance to Gideon (Jdg. 6:40).

Gideon calls an army and 32,000 men show up. That's a lot of people, but remember, they didn't have any weapons. Their arsenal probably consisted of a few sticks. Then somebody probably did the math, "There are 32,000 of us but there are 135,000 Midianites. We're outnumbered four to one!" Then God says, "Gideon, we've got a problem here." Gideon says, "You'd better believe it, we need more men!"

Please understand that sometimes endurance is tested in circumstances that seem utterly foolish. You'll find yourself asking, "Can this be God?" You'd better believe it. Look, if you can take care of everything by yourself, then you'll never develop faith or trust (Jdg. 7:2). Not only that, God will never be glorified through your circumstances. When God shows up you will be vindicated and, more importantly, He will be glorified.

Gideon is outnumbered four to one. He'd feel a whole lot better with a couple of howitzers but that's not going to happen. Instead, he's got a ragtag army of 32,000 men against 135,000 Midianites. These are the guys who swept across the land like locusts. The situation looks utterly foolish, but this is when Gideon has to endure.

Is it God? Yes.

Gideon has been commissioned by the Angel of the LORD and he's done the fleece thing, twice. It doesn't matter how many men show up for the battle, which is exactly the point God is about to make. It was God who called Gideon, and it was God who said, "Gideon, we're going to get this right. Tell everyone who is afraid to go home," (Jdg. 7:3). Can you believe it?! You're outnumbered four to one, you have no weapons, and you tell everyone who is afraid to go home.

Is this God?! Yes!

Again, this is when Gideon (and we) must endure. There may be fear and there may be uncertainty. Good! If we're paying attention, those very things will prompt dependency. Without dependency, without a sense that we need God, we'll never seek Him. There was already good reason to be afraid, and then 22,000 men went home. Now the odds are getting really foolish—try about 13:1—and still no weapons.

I challenge you to endure through fear. I will never forget the fear of turning my world upside down to start a teaching ministry. Our family had no nest egg, no support, no church sponsor, and no one who really understood my vision to begin with. Nobody was inviting me to come speak at their church, and I had to provide for three children and a wife. I thought to myself, "Dear God!" And, I wasn't the only one thinking that way.

As we moved our family from California to Oregon we stopped to visit my parents for Thanksgiving. After the weekend, we prepared for the next leg of our journey. That morning I remember walking around the truck and trailer that contained all of our worldly possessions. As I rounded a corner I saw my father by the side of the trailer. He was doubled over in pain. I rushed up and said, "Dad, what's wrong?" He replied, "Oh Roger, whenever I think of you moving back to Oregon with nothing it just causes my gut to ache." I comforted him with a sympathetic, "Oh Dad," but I was thinking, *I don't need this right now!* I mean, you don't want your father doubled over in pain because of your life's vision. That was one of the moments I had to endure. That was part of the process. God hadn't asked my father to pick up his life and start a new journey. God had given me the vision, and He had given me the grace. The only question was whether I would endure. Could I endure the questions and the fear?

God tells Gideon, "We're about to get this right. I tell ya what, Gideon. I want you to send all of your 10,000 men down to the creek and I want you to tell them to drink. Watch them. Everyone who bends over and laps like a dog, you keep. Everyone who kneels and lifts the water to his lips, you send home." Gideon watches. Do you know what he sees? He sees 9,700 observant soldiers who are kneeling and lifting the water to their lips. Scattered here and there, he sees 300 men lapping like dogs: his chosen ones. First he lost 22,000 men who had enough common sense to be afraid, and then he lost 9,700 men who had enough common sense to guard their backsides. He was left with a paltry army of 300 lapping men. It was not the most impressive army, but that's who God gave him.

There are different readings of this story. Some interpreters believe that God gave Gideon the most observant soldiers. Others (like myself) believe that God left him with the least impressive soldiers. Regardless, the point of the story is the same: Gideon wasn't supposed to depend on men, even good men. He was supposed to depend on God. I'm telling you, guys, sometimes we have to deal with circumstances and situations that seem utterly foolish. Gideon probably watched his strongest and most competent warriors go home.

Was it God? Yes.

God says, "Finally, we got it right." If you've run the numbers, you realize that the odds are about 450:1. God has pitted Gideon and 300 lapping men against 135,000 Midianite soldiers. Realize, God is (obviously) not asking Gideon to do the fighting. He is asking for faithful obedience. He is asking for endurance. How do we know? Look again how God graciously grants assurance.

Just before Gideon's brain freezes from the mind-numbing odds stacked against him, God says, "Get up! Go get 'em! I have given you the Midianite camp. But if you are still afraid, take your servant and go spy out the camp, then your hands will be strengthened to go down against them," (Jdg. 7:9-11). Gideon and his servant hike down to the outskirts of Camp Midian. They hear a couple of soldiers engaged in some intense dream analysis. They learn that God has already struck the fear of Gideon into the hearts of Midian. All of a sudden, things look a bit brighter. All of a sudden, once fearful Gideon is ready to pick a fight with his pack of 300 .

From this point forward, we hear nothing more from God. We hear no instructions nor any assurance. From this point forward, Gideon directs the show. The so-called mighty warrior summoned by the Angel of the LORD suddenly finds his strength. Gideon gets bold. Gideon gets downright audacious. Facing odds of 450:1, he decides that he's going to divide and conquer (Jdg. 7:16). Not only that, he decides the only weapons will be trumpets, torches, and empty pitchers (Jdg. 7:16). If not for God's many previous assurances, we'd be wondering why he also doesn't instruct his men to draw big targets on their chests and light up the targets with their torches. Why not end this show quickly? Gideon no longer has such fears. Is the plan foolish? Absolutely. Is God with him? You bet. Do not read this story as an excuse to avoid good planning. However, as Apostle Paul reminds the church, one of God's specialties is turning foolishness into wisdom (1Cor. 1:20).

When I started this teaching ministry, I called numerous pastors to discuss a teaching series on gender. My phone calls were usually received with a lot of skepticism. Pastors (the interested ones) generally replied:

"Gender? What about gender?"

"Well, that's what the teaching series is all about. I discuss how we develop character uniquely as men and women of God."

"Really? Well, we've already had a lot of marriage seminars."

"No, it's not a marriage seminar."

"Oh, then what's it about?"

"Gender."

At this point I could almost hear the pastor's thoughts, *That's dumb.* He'd say, "Really? How do you deal with gender?" "Well, I talk about outward/inward orientations, achievement and security needs." The pastor would cut in, "We're booked for the rest of the year."

Needless to say, the cards weren't stacked in my favor. This was the early 1980s. Gender wasn't a real hot topic. In my denomination, people were focused on faith movements and prosperity teaching. Most folks wanted to hear that a brand new Cadillac was just a prayer away. Here I was talking about character growth and death to self. Any good marketing agent (which, thankfully, I couldn't even come close to affording) could have told me that I was out of touch, out of tune, and probably out of luck. Silly me. In addition to topical irrelevance, my method was also all wrong. Traveling teachers weren't exactly the rage. Traveling evangelists? Sure. Traveling musicians? Lovely. Traveling teachers? Fat chance. On top of everything else, I didn't even have a shiny belt or spiffy white shoes to attract attention. I was in a really bad position. It seemed utterly foolish. It was almost as foolish as trumpets and torches, but it was God's call on my life. He simply asked me to endure.

Gideon's army blows the trumpets, smashes the pitchers, and waves the torches. They cry, "A sword for the LORD and for Gideon!" (Jdg. 7:20). The Midianites stream from their tents in the middle of the night. Thinking they have been surrounded, they start fighting against each other and 120,000

Midianites are killed! Gideon and his men can smell blood. They may have lost the element of surprise, they may have lost the cover of night, and they may still be outnumbered 50:1—no matter! Gideon and his 300 warriors set off after the remaining 15,000 Midianites.

Is it God? Yes.

Gideon's army passes through a couple of small villages. At each stop Gideon says, "Give us some bread. We're suffering. We need help. We're going to finish off the Midianites." Think about this for just a second. These villagers had just seen 15,000 Midianite soldiers mowing down their flower-beds. Before the dust can even settle, they see this little pack of 300 cub scouts who seem all intent about some do-gooder mission. How would you have responded? "Whoa, I don't think so." I mean this is like a chihuahua chasing a rottweiler. But, is it God? Yes. Long before Arnold Schwarzenegger coins the famous phrase, Gideon says, "I'll be back." And he does come back. He punishes the elders from one village with thorns and briers. He tears down a tower and kills the men of another village (Jdg. 8:16,17).

I don't care how many great things you accomplish. There will always be a new step of faith. You have to endure. People will say things like, "You just lucked out last time. This time you'll eat your lunch. Fat chance." Every time we approach a step of faith, we have to ask, "Is it God?" God's presence, His gracious assurance is the only thing that can possibly allow us to endure in the face of the world's assault.

Now we come to the twenty-second verse of the eighth chapter of the book of Judges. The men of Israel come to Gideon and say, "Rule over us, both you and your son, also your son's son, for you have delivered us from the hand of Midian." Gideon replies, "No, I will not rule over you." Was that God? Yes. "Yet...I would request of you, that each of you give me an earring from his spoil." A little thing. No big deal. Was that God? No.

Gideon took the spoils and crafted an ephod, a priestly garment used to inquire of God. From outward appearances, Gideon was redirecting the people to God. He was pointing them to their true deliverer, and their true king. But is that what he was really doing? No. He hung the ephod on the wall of his city and Israel played the harlot (Jdg. 8:27). They worshiped the gift, not the Giver. It led them to destruction. It was just a little thing at the very end, but Gideon didn't endure. He had seventy sons. His posterity was incredibly blessed, yet after his death one of his sons slaughtered sixty-eight of his brothers on a rock in a single day. The wicked son, Abimelech, himself died in bloody shame (Jdg.

9:53), leaving but one son of Gideon's posterity. Just a little thing, but Gideon didn't endure and the result was tragic.

No matter where you find yourself on this journey of life, you must learn to endure. When you recognize God's presence, when you hear His call, and when you see His sovereignty, know that you will be called to endure. As sure as winds bring rain (Prov. 25:23), God's call demands endurance. Not only that, full obedience entails willing consent for God to act in His time and in His way. Be thankful for those moments. Be thankful that you can depend on God and not logic, reason, or strength. Depend on God. You must endure.

In the previous chapter I discussed our daughter's death. Julie was a marvelous blessing and we miss her daily. I often think of the final days I spent with my daughter. They happened during the third week of March, 1984. It was less than one year after I started my traveling ministry. I had been hitting the trail pretty hard. I had been gone most of the month. On this week, like many others, I came home on Thursday and I would leave again on Saturday. Elaine brought the kids to the airport when she came to pick me up. It happened to be Spring Break in Oregon. Elaine told me that we were going to spend a day at the zoo and the Oregon Museum of Science. We were going to spend a day with the kids and just have some fun. I said, "Great."

We drove to the zoo and discovered that a lot of other families had the same idea. We began searching for parking and ended up way out in the boondocks. It was practically wilderness. In the spirit of Lewis and Clark we began our long trek towards the zoo (probably 200-300 yards). Like Lewis and Clark, we knew we would face wild animals. Unlike Lewis and Clark, our wild animals were securely behind bars (hey, you've got to find some way to add a little adventure when you're in a parking lot). Elaine and the (robust, healthy) boys began skipping along. I noticed that Julie was lagging a few paces behind our merry band of travelers. I had no way of knowing that she was less than nine days from death. In little more than one week, her heart would fail from consistent, chronic resistance in the blood vessels of her lungs.

Julie's condition literally robbed her body of stamina. It robbed her of physical endurance. The demands of daily existence placed incredible stress on her heart. Any thoughts of prolonged running, jumping, or childish skipping were just that—childish dreams. Recognizing the situation but not wanting to make an issue of it, I walked back and slid my arm around her. I had missed her during my trip. I pulled her tight to my side and lifted her up. Like any good thirteen-year-old girl, she went, "Dad!" I said, "Don't worry about it, babe." We walked together, side-by-side as the saying goes. She sort of bumped me and goofed around and I said, "It's okay. I can get you there." I could feel her heart beating so hard against my side. I look back and think, *Dear God...if only I had known.*

Nine days later, on Saturday, March 31st I remember screaming at God, "Why would you do this to me?!" How could this be God? At 2:00 a.m. I stood at a window, staring into the darkness and screaming in my heart, *God, if you raise the sun I'll never preach again!* (God was really nervous, what would He do?!) As many of you know, the sun indeed rose that day. It was April 1st, April Fool's Day no less. Talk about a divine slap in the face. I was convinced that this could not be the work of God. I wanted my daughter back! Yes, it was selfish and self-centered to want her back when she was with God. Nevertheless, I wanted my daughter. Was this God? Yes. He numbers every day before we take our first breath (Psa. 139). Julie's death wasn't meaningless and it wasn't random. I could still trust God, and I could still trust His call on my life. God was still God.

When I look back on that spring afternoon, when I think about bearing Julie's weight across that parking lot, I cannot help but think of that famous poem, "Footprints In The Sand." As the narrator looks back and surveys the sands of life, as he recalls the good times and the bad, he notices something odd. In the trying times and during difficult circumstances he sees only one set of footprints in the sand. Confused and wounded, the narrator asks, "God, why did you abandon me when I needed you most?" God's answer is very simple, "My child, I love you and I would never abandon you. During those trying times when you see only one set of footprints, it was then that I carried you."

Remember Paul. Here was a man who wrote at least half of the New Testament. Yet, he was imprisoned, faced countless floggings, and was often near death. "Five times I received from the Jews thirty-nine lashes. Three times I was beaten with rods, once I was stoned, three times I was shipwrecked, a night and a day I have spent in the deep. I have been on frequent journeys, in dangers from rivers, dangers from robbers, dangers from my countrymen, dangers from the Gentiles, dangers in the city, dangers in the wilderness, dangers on the sea, dangers among false brethren; I have been in labor and hardship, through many sleepless nights, in hunger and thirst, often without food, in cold and exposure," (2Cor. 11:24-27). On top of all this, he spent the last days of his life in a dark, wet hole. He could surely hear the bustling city above him reveling in all of its wealth and glory. In the midst of all this he could say, "I have run my race. I have finished my course." That is a picture of godly endurance.

Finish well. I say again, finish well.

5

ENDURANCE IN WOMEN: TRUST AND HOPE IN GOD

Then the Lord took note of Sarah as He had said, and the Lord did for Sarah as He had promised. So Sarah conceived and bore a son to Abraham in his old age, at the appointed time of which God had spoken to him. And Abraham called the name of his son who was born to him, whom Sarah bore to him, Isaac....And Sarah said, "God has made laughter for me; everyone who hears will laugh with me."

~ Genesis 21:1-3,6

After one of my (multiple) eye surgeries, Elaine drove me to the hospital for the all-important results. If Hollywood had composed a score for this occasion, the music would have begun softly and built to a crescendo. There was drama. There was tension. This was a big moment. After several previous surgeries, things were starting to look bleak—literally. A cataract had been removed but my vision hadn't improved. In fact, it had actually gotten worse. We were facing one of two possibilities. Either temporary effects from the latest surgery were obstructing my vision, or my optic nerve was ruined. Doctors held out hope but they were basically playing a guessing game. Their best guess was that maybe the sutures securing my eye's new lens (yet a different surgery) were distorting the shape of my eye and affecting my vision. Now, it was time to test that theory. Now, two months after the latest surgery, doctors could measure my eye and loosen the sutures if necessary. Everyone was hoping and praying that a solution was still at hand, hoping that doctors could help me regain some vision, hoping that I would not be legally blind. With sufficient treatment, someday I might even be able to sit on the driver's-side of the car again. All of these thoughts were running through my head as we drove to the hospital.

When the doctor entered the room he just shook his head. It was one of those moments when nothing could be done. He said, "Nope. Your eye has a normal shape. That's not the problem." In other words, my optic nerve was shot. The kicker is that I have since lost the other nerve. Both optic nerves are essentially gone. No matter how much light enters my eyes, no matter how sharply the images are focused on either retina, most of the information never reaches my brain. The pathway, the nerve, has been crushed. My options are pretty slim. Aside from God's healing I'm stuck like this until the medical establishment solicits volunteers for experimental head transplants. It's not something I expect anytime soon.

Needless to say, the prognosis was disappointing. Actually, it was downright crushing. However, I wasn't just sorry for myself. This was no individual pity party. As I peered across the room and recognized the shadowy figure that I knew was my wife, I tried to understand what this meant for her. We were in this together. We were joined at the hip. My handicap was more than a nuisance. It was her handicap as well.

Elaine has since told me that she felt a sense of fear and despair. She was afraid that I would not be able to work any longer. How could I continue to get around airports, let alone read and study the materials needed for my teaching? She was also afraid of the unknown. How would my disability impact our life together? With all of these fears in her heart we suddenly found ourselves back in the hospital a few months later for another surgery. This time it was an emergency.

I will let Elaine describe the episode in her own words:

> On a Sunday morning we drove from Salem to Portland for Roger to speak at a church. He had scheduled an urgent appointment with the eye doctor before going to church. When the specialist checked Roger's eye he said, "You only have a few hours left before the cornea detaches from that right eye and you lose your vision. You go do your speech. I will get the operating team together and then we'll do the surgery."
>
> As I sat in the waiting room, unsure of the outcome, I remember feeling like I was the only soul in that entire building. It was Sunday so all the other offices and reception areas were closed. After rushing Roger from the eye institute and then to church and back, I found myself sitting in this

barren room. As I sat there, the tears began to flow. I felt an overpowering need to talk with my adult sons, who were living in the Midwest. When I phoned Greg, my eldest son, I could hardly talk because I was so filled with emotion. Greg's love and comfort helped ease my pain, but I was still gripped with fear. The same thing happened when I talked with Eric, my youngest son. Again, I felt love and comfort but the fear remained.

Within a few days of the emergency surgery, we were thankful to learn that Roger hadn't lost all his vision. However, a few weeks later we were crushed to learn that he was nonetheless legally blind. His optic nerve wasn't totally destroyed, but it was significantly tattered and crushed. His field of vision was too patchy and dim to drive, read, or even navigate the dips and curves of our neighborhood sidewalk. We were immediately introduced to a whole host of "misses"—both concrete and abstract—in our daily lives. As we faced this unfamiliar future, I was so glad I had learned to anchor my hope and trust in the Lord after the life and loss of my daughter. I was painfully reminded that I often don't have a choice about the events that happen to me and my loved ones, but I can choose to place my trust in the Lord. He has been so faithful!

As I witnessed in Elaine, endurance may not feel especially demanding when life is going well. The call to hope and trust just doesn't feel so urgent when the answers for daily situations seem clear. During the smooth seasons of life, it may become very easy to rely on individual insight and awareness. However, in God's gracious love, He allows enough momentary light affliction to produce in us "an eternal weight of glory" (2Cor. 4:17). The cycle of affliction continually draws us back to Him, even though we may feel like screaming, "Enough glory already!"

From an early age, women begin to feel the impact of a father and/or other influential men in their lives. God has called men to reflect His own love and character in these relationships. However, men inevitably fall short of this rather tall order. The pervasive effects of repeated pain and loss make it all too easy for young women to learn a deep distrust of men and God alike: "Why would God let this happen to me?" "I can't even begin to think of God as a caring father!" "Love just doesn't work." At these painful moments women are called to place their hope and trust in God instead of man. God becomes the means to endurance. In her book, "The Hiding Place," Corrie ten Boom, a Dutch clockmaker's daughter who survived a Nazi concentration camp during World War II, said, "I know that the experiences of our lives, when we let God use them, become the mysterious and perfect preparation for the work He will give us to do." This quote clearly articulates the heart of Christian trust.

Contemporary Western culture pressures women to resist vulnerability and conditions them to view interpersonal attachments as conditional arrangements. These cultural forces make it incredibly difficult for women to place any sort of meaningful hope and trust in their relationships. It has become downright counter-cultural for women and men alike to experience relationships as safe places to nurture long-term meaning and identity. In this cultural climate, how much more difficult it must be to hope and trust in the God who surrounds women with flawed and muddled men. Hope may even begin to feel like a sick joke. What a profound loss! Hope encourages. It builds up. It is willing to reach outside of itself. True hope facilitates endurance: "We also exult in our tribulations, knowing that tribulation brings about perseverance; and perseverance, proven character, and proven character, hope; and hope does not disappoint, because the love of God has been poured out within our hearts, through the Holy Spirit who was given to us," (Romans 5:2-5). True hope doesn't disappoint! True hope, Biblical hope doesn't disappoint because God's love is poured out in our hearts. We find security in God's love as we hope and trust with endurance.

I have often pondered the similarities and contrasts between the matriarchs of Judaism and Christianity. I am fascinated by the lives of Sarah and Mary. Their experiences are amazing. However, even more amazing is what God achieved in, through, and sometimes in spite of them. In Sarah's life, God worked directly with Abraham and she had to adjust. In Mary's life, God dealt directly with her, and Joseph had to adjust. In each and every instance, God was most glorified when these ladies endured in their hope and trust. When endurance wavered, tragedy ensued. Their lives continue to teach and encourage us today.

We meet Sarah in the book of Genesis. Among other things, we learn that she is barren (Gen. 16:1). This is important for several reasons. First, it is important for all of the cultural and emotional reasons discussed in chapter three (see the story of Naomi and Ruth). Put simply, barrenness was a social blight. It meant that Sarah was deficient. Moreover, it was an emotional burden. Motherhood was and is a God-given yearning and desire. Sarah not only lacked the social standing conferred by childbirth, she also missed the joy and fulfillment of family life. She did not have the nurturing and sharing that accompanies such intimate community. The reality of Sarah's suffering is summarized in her euphemism for childbirth: to have pleasure (Gen. 18:12).

Let's also think about this barrenness in the context of Sarah's age. At this point in the story both Sarah and Abraham are, shall we say, well aged. Their barrenness is no passing phase. Sarah is seventy-five years old and Abraham is eighty-five years old. Under normal circumstances Sarah should have long since had her own grandchildren, even great-grandchildren. Yet it will still be fifteen years before she becomes a mother at the age of ninety, an age where it clearly should have "ceased to be with Sarah after the manner of women," (Gen. 18:11—NRSV). Finally, this barrenness is important because God has already promised to make Abraham's offspring as numerous as the stars (Gen. 15:5). Not only a social blight, not only an emotional burden, not only reinforced by the reality of old age, this barrenness seems to directly contradict the promises of God.

Needless to say, this is a problem for Sarah and Abraham. Sarah is barren. This is seemingly an act of God, yet God has promised that Abraham's offspring will be a great nation. The tension isn't lost on either Sarah or Abe. In fact, Abraham poses the problem to God quite bluntly (Gen. 15:2-3). From our vantage point, we can read ahead in the story to see God's plan, His altogether gracious provision. God not only noticed and understood Sarah's barrenness, He intended to use it for His glory. Sarah and Abraham didn't have the luxury of reading ahead. They were simply asked to hope, to trust, and to be faithful. We are asked nothing less.

Ladies, you can face many types of barrenness in your life. No matter what form your emptiness takes, don't ever fall into the trap of thinking that God doesn't care. God does care and has a plan for you (Jer. 29:11-12). You may be given promises that are not delivered—in marriage, with children, in the workplace, and even in church. Please endure with hope and trust in Him. God knows. God cares.

Many years after God's promise was given, Sarah felt compelled to take matters into her own hands and offered Hagar as a substitute matriarch for Abraham's promised lineage (Gen. 16:2). These seeds of distrust eventually reaped a harvest of sorrow for Sarah and Hagar alike (Gen. 16:5-6). Finally, when Sarah was eighty-nine years old, the Lord reappeared and confirmed his intention to provide a child of promise (Gen. 18:10). Imperfect as she was, Sarah did experience the fulfilled promise of her own son with Abraham. At the birth of Isaac, her barrenness was erased. After years of struggling to preserve her hope and trust in God, she finally experienced the fulfillment. Imperfect as she was, she endured and was able to say, "God has brought me laughter, and everyone who hears about this will laugh with me" (Gen. 21:6).

In some ways, Mary's situation was the exact opposite of Sarah's. Young Mary was just minding her own business one day when the Angel of the Lord suddenly appeared, "Hail, highly favored one!" (Luke 1:28). That kind of greeting would certainly make you wonder what was coming next.

"Don't be afraid. You're going to give birth to a son."

"How can this be, since I am a virgin?"

"Don't worry, we'll take care of everything."

Can you imagine what that was like, ladies? Mary was probably between twelve and fifteen years old. She lived in a culture that was extremely protective of a woman's virginity. How protective? They were protective to the point of burying violators under a pile of rocks (Deut. 22:21). Suddenly, without any physical involvement, Mary was pregnant. Pregnant! Can you imagine? On the one hand, incredible joy. On the other hand, incredible fear. What could she say? What could she do? Her response: "May it be done to me according to your word." (Luke 1:38). Incredible. The time had come to endure.

Ladies, sometimes God calls you to similar forms of patient endurance. Maybe he provides insight. Maybe He grants understanding. Maybe you can understand a situation better than anyone else but you can't say a word. You have knowledge, ability, and understanding but if you address the situation on your own terms you will totally compromise your position. Someone might even look down on you or think you're prideful. Maybe you feel like you can't even say anything to your friends, because if you open that door who knows where it will lead. How do you deal with these kinds of situations?

Sometimes stewardship of God-given insight demands action. It demands that you step forward, that you stand in the gap and endure the consequences come what may. Other times, God will grant insight and simply ask you to trust Him. Sometimes good stewardship will mean that you quietly intercede. The challenging thing is when God grants insight, when He reveals the heart of your friends or co-workers, your family or church, and He calls you first and foremost to be an intercessor. When that happens, be the one who endures. Be the one who runs the good race, who finishes the course. Your heart may cry out, "I don't want to deal with this! Why would God treat me like this?!" I'm sure Mary had similar moments.

Immediately after the angel left, "Mary arose and went with haste to the hill country...and entered the house of Zacharias and greeted Elizabeth" (Luke

1:39-40). In contrast to Sarah's less direct dealings with God, Mary has heard from God directly thorough an angel. Notice how God provides the means for enduring hope and trust. First, Mary hears the angel say, "Nothing will be impossible with God" (Luke 1:37). Next, she hears from the Holy Spirit through Elizabeth, "Blessed among women are you, and blessed is the fruit of your womb!" (Luke 1:42). Mary's response to Elizabeth is framed in the form of a prayer offering, "The Mighty One has done great things for me; and holy is His name" (Luke 1:49). As Mary and Elizabeth shared the next three months together, I can imagine a building sense of joy and excitement. Elizabeth was drawing closer to her time of delivery while Mary began to embrace the reality of her pregnancy.

"And Mary ... returned to her home" (Luke 1:56). This is where Mary's true test began, when she found herself face-to-face with her real world. She had left "with haste" and returned three months later—pregnant! The village was surely buzzing. We don't know how she broke the news to Joseph but we do read about his response. "Not wanting to disgrace her, (he) desired to put her away secretly" (Matt 1:19). I wonder if her family felt the same way. It took another angelic visit to convince Joseph that her story checked out. He eventually embraced Mary in marital support.

"Mary treasured up all these things, pondering them in her heart" (Luke 2:19). When God deals directly with a woman, her memory of the "message" may turn out to be the most important source of enduring hope and trust. Mary held on to the memory of God's message in her life. When Jesus was twelve years old, he decided not to join the family travel plans and spent some extra time in Jerusalem. Mary and Joseph finally found him, "sitting in the midst of the teachers, both listening to them and asking them questions. And all who heard Him were amazed at His understanding and His answers" (Luke 2:46–47). In the midst of her certain concern and exasperation, we again find Mary "treasuring all these things in her heart" (Luke 2:51). There would be eighteen more years before Jesus launched his Kingdom ministry, culminating in his own death and resurrection. At the foot of the cross, we again witness God's enduring love and concern as Jesus commends his mother to the beloved disciple (John 19:26-27). God does care.

Over the years, Elaine and I have both wrestled with endurance as we daily learn to live with the death of our daughter. Elaine expresses this journey quite well:

It's been a long and difficult journey walking towards healing from
the death of our daughter, Julie. At times I thought I'd arrived, only to
discover there was something new to surrender to the Lord about this special
relationship. I can earnestly say with Job, that the Lord gives and the Lord
takes away, but blessed be the name of the Lord (Job 1:21). Six years after
her death, as a part of this journey, I felt compelled to write my daughter a
letter. It is an affirmation of endurance. I've entitled it, "Julie, Goodbye".

"Julie, I didn't know on that Saturday in March, 1984, a day that seemed the same as a multitude of others, that this would be your last. It would be not only your last Saturday, but your last day - ever. You were exactly thirteen years and four months old.

I remember what a bright, healthy-looking infant you were; you weighed nine pounds and twelve ounces when you were born. When you turned blue on your second day, the nurse placed you in an incubator and your head touched one end and your toes the other. Within a few months the doctors detected a heart murmur, and you had surgery to close your peyton-ductus valve, but were left with pulmonary hypertension. As the years passed, I remember explaining to you that the pressures between your heart and lungs were five times more than "normal." However, as the doctor said, we didn't know what was normal for your heart, or what it would be able to take. As a pediatric cardiologist, his prognosis for you was twenty to thirty years, the same as all the other physicians, except the one in San Francisco. He predicted twelve years. We didn't like him and never saw him again. That Saturday night in March was to prove him the most accurate.

I want you to know that I have learned much from that day. I'm sure you sensed the fear in me in the evening; but I'm glad the day was typical. I believe it represents a microcosm of our life together. The joys, the frustrations, the love, the pain, the learning to grow together, they were all there; in other words, we were living life to the fullest at its richest and best. I witnessed a maturity and love in you that day that is still beyond my understanding. You lived, you died, and you left behind a legacy of caring and love that grows as the years pass.

I didn't know love was like that. I also didn't know that love could hurt so much. That night I understood shock, confronted the painful denial of your death, tried to bargain with God, and learned that anger is a part of grief. As a parent, I also learned in one short evening that all the years of teaching, training, nurturing and loving really do "payoff." As a mother of three adolescents, I sometimes wondered. Your will, left in your "secret box," was evidence of your joy with life, love of your friends and family, and your acceptance of God's direction for your life, an acceptance that has taken me many years to achieve. As I remember the day you left, it is with new hope.

That day. Dad was in a motel room in Ohio getting ready for a church seminar that would begin on Sunday. I had awakened and occupied myself with making pancakes while the happy sounds of cartoons rose from the television in the living room. We were still finishing the last of breakfast, when Michelle phoned to invite you for a day of shopping and movies with her family. I didn't want you to go, because you still had your household chores to do. However, the pleading look in your eyes, combined with the earnest promise that the house would be dusted before you went to bed, won your case. You were not able to keep that promise, but I'm glad that I had learned the value of taking time to develop friendships; especially at the expense of the mundane. The house has "demanded" to be dusted many times since then, but that was to be your last day with your best friend.

As the day progressed, your brothers and I vacuumed the carpets, mopped the linoleum, scoured the bathrooms, and washed the dirty laundry. In fact, the house looked so good, I decided to take Greg and Eric to the movies as a reward for a job well done. We drove to the Albany Cinema, purchased tickets, and waited for the early afternoon performance to finish. To our surprise, you and Michelle came out of the same theater we were entering. After visiting for a while, we went into the theater and you left with Michelle's family.

When I arrived home with Greg and Eric, you were in bed. You had gotten sick on the way home from Albany. Your elevated pulse was typical of what I'd seen many times. I thought with a little rest you'd be fine. However, I sensed a fear in you and decided not to leave you alone. The boys were hungry, so I ordered a pizza instead of taking the time to cook. As the evening wore on, your pulse didn't come down. I began to get worried and tried to phone your cardiologist in Portland. She wasn't available, but I talked with a cardiologist at the Health Sciences Center who recommended an injection to relieve the nausea you were experiencing. I had to work through our local family doctor, who recommended I take you to the emergency room at Good Samaritan Hospital. I also phoned Dad to let him know what was happening.

All my phoning took a couple hours. It was a Saturday night, the doctors weren't in, and I had to do a lot of waiting for return calls. During this time you were getting more and more listless. I kept checking your pulse, talked with you, prayed with you, read Psalms 90 and 91, and made sure Greg or Eric were with you if I had to leave your room. I also remember turning on the radio at your request. Just before we were ready to take you to the hospital for your injection, you threw-up. Greg and I tried to carry you up the stairs to the garage, but you were so limp Greg offered to carry you. As he reached the top of the steps and opened the door to the garage he screamed, "She's not breathing!" I had him lay you down on the floor of the entryway, kneeling beside you and holding your head in my lap. I had never seen you so still in all my life; you weren't breathing. I remember the frantic thought, "Where's she gone?" Panic gripped my heart and mind. I will never forget what seemed like an independent thought, separate from my own, which dropped into my mind and said, "Tell her to start breathing." I said, "Julie, breathe; Jesus loves you." Slowly you drew in a deep breath. I kept repeating that phrase, and slowly you kept breathing.

In the meantime, Greg had phoned the emergency number, and the fire truck with the medics arrived in three minutes. They worked on you for about ten minutes in our home. I remember how crowded our entryway was with all of them trying to help. I have wondered what it seemed like to you. I felt myself starting to shake uncontrollably as I backed up our stairs to make room for them. I remember shaking my head and heard myself saying, "You won't stop working on her, you won't stop working on her." Someone said, "No, we won't." Several of the medics looked up at me. One of them nodded towards me, and a man came up the steps and held my elbow. It helped having someone touch me; it kept me in touch with reality.

I have since had a new, practical compassion for people going through trauma. I have learned the importance of touch. Physical contact makes the unreal seem real, even if only in a remote way, while an individual is in shock.

While I was standing on the steps shaking, the man next to me said that we were going to the hospital with you now. I asked if I could ride in the ambulance with them. They said I could, but there wasn't room for the boys. I told Greg and Eric to phone Pastor Griffin and have him bring them to the hospital. I then asked the medic if I should take my purse. One of the ladies in the group said that I should. I couldn't make even a simple decision. They didn't allow me to ride with you in the back of the ambulance; I had to ride in the front with the driver.

When we arrived at the hospital, they wheeled you into the emergency room immediately. I never saw you alive again. The hospital attendants had our family and the two ministers with their wives wait in a small room. Our family doctor came in and said that you weren't doing very well; they were having trouble getting you to breathe. It was at that time I was reminded by our pastor to phone dad. We were on the phone praying with the boys when our doctor reentered and said that you had died. Shock and denial were strong in me. I remember thinking, *No, this can't be, we're supposed to have another ten to twenty years with you!* It seemed like a bad dream; my mind felt detached from my body. Our doctor asked if Greg, Eric and I wanted to see you. We said that we did. When we arrived at the door to your room, we looked in, and Greg and Eric both said they didn't want to go in; they thought you looked blue.

I walked into your room by myself and started shaking again. You didn't look blue to me; you looked perfect. You looked like you should stand up and come home. I remember sitting beside you and touching you. Your body already felt cold and stiff. I decided to touch and stroke your hair because it still felt like you. I remember saying, "Oh, Julie!" as I wept. Both Greg and Eric said they could hear me wailing in the hall where they were waiting. I remember first asking God to heal you; you looked so perfect. Nothing happened. I then remember telling God that I had had a full life; would He take mine and give you back yours? Still, nothing happened. Then I remember the anger I felt. I remember shaking my fist at an upper corner in the room. In my mind's eye, I could see Him standing there holding you by the hand. The only thing I could think to say was, "You'd better take good care of her!"

I have since learned that the emotions I experienced are very typical of the death and dying process. Dr. Elisabeth Kubler-Ross, in her now famous study, relates that the five stages of death are denial, anger, bargaining, depression and acceptance. I experienced three of them in a very short time. The process doesn't have to come in this order, and even though you've worked through it once, it can cycle back around, especially with grief.

As Greg, Eric and I were leaving the hospital, with only your slippers in hand, one of the boys said, "Mama, did you know that Julie left a will?" I was surprised and responded, "No, I didn't. Where is it?" They said they would get it when we got home. I couldn't believe it, Julie! In your desk was a little container on which you'd written "Secret Box." Of course, your brothers knew exactly where it was. Inside, neatly folded, lay your words of comfort, hope, and encouragement to us. It was laced with your unique humor. You had written it on March second, just twenty-nine days before your death. In the process of writing it, you showed me that you had accepted what I could not. You outlined your funeral, and ended your will with, "God bless each and every one of you. I always wanted to say that. Remember John 3:16."

Your will demonstrated to me that every minute I invested in your life has been overwhelmingly worthwhile. Your maturity, your attitudes, your joy and humor, your love for your family and friends, your faith in God and acceptance of what you were "handed" in life; these all show me the manner in which you accepted your training and discipline, grew from it in understanding, and then grew beyond it in application. That's maturity. Most parents aren't able to witness this progression in their children's lives until they're well into adulthood. Your life was condensed, but complete in just thirteen short years. This has strengthened my belief in careful and consistent parenting, combined with a faith in God. There were times when I wondered if it was worth the financial and professional sacrifices for me to stay home as much as I did, in order to give the time we felt was necessary for your personal development. I don't question that anymore.

One of the main areas of concern I had for you as a parent was that of your spiritual growth. We were never able to have our family devotions that night, but if I could have that evening back with you there, I would read from Romans 5:3-5, "but we also rejoice in our sufferings, because we know that suffering produces perseverance; perseverance, character; and character, hope. And hope does not disappoint us, because God has poured out his love into our hearts by the Holy Spirit, whom he has given us." Hope has replaced the anger and depression. With hope has come an understanding; not of your death, I know I'll never understand that. What I can understand is myself. With God's help, I'm attempting to correct personality and character flaws that go back decades, and trying to develop new abilities for the future. I'm working at making myself useful, to myself, to others, and to God. At one time I thought the emotions of my loss would destroy me. I've chosen to turn them into a drive to excel. At times I'm fearful, but that's a lot better than being angry or bitter. The fears let me know that I'm growing or pushing myself. As I've experienced healing during the last six years since your death, there's been a sweetness added to the diminishing pain that I can only describe as "bittersweet." The bitter part is the void that will always be there by your absence. The sweetness is the joy I have in knowing that because of your love, you are a part of my very character, a permanent part of who I am. I've also discovered that I'll be telling you "good bye" for the rest of my life. Not that I haven't already said, "good bye" to you. That farewell was to the budding adolescent girl; I must now say "good bye" to the young college woman. Someday it will be to the young wife and mother, and on and on it will go. Each stage of life will have its own farewell to that particular set of hopes and dreams. And so, daughter, I say, "Julie, goodbye; goodbye to the young woman I will never know."

6

PASSION IN MEN:
EMOTIONAL ROLLER-COASTER OR
DETERMINED OBEDIENCE

In the days of Herod, king of Judea, there was a priest named Zacharias,
of the division of Abijah; and he had a wife from the daughters of Aaron,
and her name was Elizabeth. They were both righteous in the sight of
God, walking blamelessly in all the commandments and requirements of
the Lord. But they had no child, because Elizabeth was barren, and they
were both advanced in years.

~ Luke 1:5-7

Passion. The word conjures up an entire world of emotion and desire. As a
concept, passion carries a life of its own. It is a living, breathing thing. Passion is
active. It has "legs." Things that we are passionate about tend to get done. Things
that we aren't passionate about tend to slide off our list of things to do.

Passion. The word reminds me of a particular story. Incredibly, it is only
one of many such stories in *Foxe's Book of Martyrs*. The book was first published
in the mid-sixteenth century and for the next one-hundred years, before the
printing of *Pilgrim's Progress,* people in the Western world had almost no reading
material other than the Bible and Foxe. The book is far from a warm and fuzzy
tale, but oh how I wish our churches would read it today. Foxe chronicles the
"triumphant deaths" of the Church's martyrs. The history is horrific, yet the
passion is pervasive. In the comfortable world of Western democracy, we can
all too easily feel detached from the world of martyrs. Such distance is more
imagined than real. I have often heard that more people died for Christ's Church

in the twentieth century than in the previous nineteen centuries combined. How have we allowed ourselves to feel so detached? More importantly, what does our detachment reveal about our passion?

Foxe recounts the story of a young couple named Timothy and Maura. They had been married but three weeks when they were separated by persecution. Imagine their passion. Timothy, a deacon of Mauritania, was summoned to appear before the governor of the region. The governor, a man named Arrianus, demanded the Scriptures from Timothy's church. They were to be surrendered for destruction. Timothy replied, "Had I children, I would sooner deliver them up to be sacrificed than part with the Word of God." Arrianus assured Timothy that the Scriptures would be of no use to him, and proceeded to remove Timothy's eyes with red-hot irons. According to Foxe, Timothy withstood the ordeal with such fortitude that the governor grew greatly exasperated. In an effort to overcome Timothy's fortitude, Arrianus strung him up by his feet, hung a weight around his neck, and stuffed a gag in his mouth. At this point Maura was ushered in to see her beloved. Can you imagine, ladies, a bride of three weeks finding her husband in such a condition? With all the language of affection (and passion!) Maura assailed Timothy's commitment to Jesus Christ. According to Foxe, when the gag was removed from Timothy's mouth, he reproved Maura for her mistaken love and reaffirmed his resolve to die for the faith. Maura not only regained her composure, she emulated Timothy's courage. She was crucified next to her husband after being severely tortured. The year was 304 A.D. Less than eight years later, Constantine conquered Rome and Christianity was released from persecution. If they had still been living, Timothy and Maura would suddenly have had the life they always dreamed of. They would have been the cute couple at church, just eight years later. But because of their circumstances and their commitment to Jesus Christ, they were killed in brutal fashion.

Passion. The underlying intensity drives us. The passion of emotion impels us forward. However, we can't live our entire lives on an emotional edge. Enthusiasm ebbs and flows. Occasionally we can even lose our passion, no matter how many medications or hormones we enlist to aid our cause. Interestingly, little things can make a big impact. A string of seemingly small annoyances can utterly consume our passion.

A few years ago I experienced a run of events that put my passion to the test. It all began with something simple. It seemed downright silly. I stepped off a curb the wrong way. For those of us who don't see very well, a curb can be a tricky thing to navigate. Thankfully I am blessed with a wife who routinely sounds the alarm—"Curb!"—when we approach a break in the sidewalk. On our visits to Europe, where the engineering is a bit different, she even alters her alarm to match the terrain. Instead of the American "Curb!" I brace myself for the European "Dip!" at the edge of a walkway. As you can imagine, I am incredibly thankful for these verbal warnings, although I'm never quite sure if "Dip!" refers to the street or to me. Anyway, my wife wasn't with me on this particular occasion and I twisted my knee. The situation was simple enough to make me feel foolish, yet serious enough to require surgery. Even so, I told myself it wasn't that big of a deal. I mean, professional athletes get injured all the time. It seems like these guys have surgery on Monday and are back making plays by Sunday. Naturally, I assumed that my body was every bit as capable. When I asked the surgeon how long recovery would take he, surely noting my age and physical condition, seemed to have a more cautious outlook. He said, "We'll see." About three months later I was still gimping around in great frustration.

During my recovery, I experienced an odd twang in my abdomen. Again, it was something simple, even silly. I just coughed one day and felt a twang. I thought it was probably a pulled muscle. I thought maybe the knee injury (right knee) affected my abdomen (right abdomen). That's about the extent of my medical knowledge. I was certain the twang would go away, but it didn't. If anything, it got worse and I began reflexively grabbing at it. One Sunday I was speaking in front of a rather large congregation. The adrenaline was flowing and I began grabbing at my abdomen. The Pastor of the church approached me afterward and was genuinely concerned that I might have appendicitis. I said, "Nah, I just got this pulled muscle." A few days later I was speaking at my home church and began experiencing even worse pain. I actually had to sit down because I thought I might pass out. Everyone kept saying, "You've got appendicitis!" I replied, "Nah, the only thing I've heard about that hurts this bad is a tubal pregnancy. It must be a tubal pregnancy—ha ha." Nobody believed me. I finally discovered that I had a hernia, or more appropriately in my case, a him-nia. Just like the knee, it was simple but it was serious. Still suffering the effects of surgery number one, I had to schedule another procedure and then brace myself for several (more!) weeks (or months!) of recovery. Just thinking about the situation began to wear me down.

We live in a sin-stained universe. None of us will schmooze through life untouched by difficulty, trial, or pain. We all suffer the effects of a phenomenon called entropy. Entropy is an unavoidable reality. Simply stated, entropy means that things run down, lose energy, and fall apart. We live in a transitory world where things grow old and die. You will never purchase something that naturally grows toward perfection. To the contrary, the passage of time reveals the opposite effect. You can spend thousands of dollars on a beautiful car that seems absolutely perfect, but it will suffer the effects of entropy. A few weeks down the road it will already have a couple of dings. As time goes on imperfections become even more obvious, glaringly obvious. We simply can't escape the physical effects of entropy no matter how hard we try.

Don't you just love it when you see a lone car parked at the far edge of a parking lot? You can almost picture the prudent (or, paranoid) owner. (S)He has gone to ridiculous extremes to maximize the natural buffer zone surrounding this precious possession. The silly car might even be positioned sideways across two parking spaces in case anyone even thinks about parking nearby. In my weaker moments, I almost want to pull right up next to the car and fling open my door with reckless abandon. "Oops!"

I don't mean to offend anyone who parks at the edge of parking lots, but we all realize that hyper-protective measures just delay the inevitable. Things grow old. Stuff fails. It's a simple matter of entropy. No matter how hard we try, we cannot escape the effects of entropy in the physical world. But wait, there's more bad news. We seem to suffer emotional entropy as well. Do you remember when you were young and you could just flit from one situation to the next? Transitions were something you actually embraced. Even when things didn't go your way, you never seemed to get too discouraged or feel too worn down. Every day was a new day. As you grow older things tend to look a bit different. When you finally manage to drag yourself out of bed, you absolutely dread going to work and you leave the office by noon because you're just so weary and frazzled. You walk into the house only to discover that your cat has vomited a hairball in the corner. The entire episode is enough to throw you into an emotional tailspin. It's just too much! Life has worn you down. You simply can't handle one more setback.

Physical and emotional entropy can also have spiritual side-effects. We begin wondering why we have all these problems. Why doesn't God step in and do something? "C'mon God, just fix it!" We all have moments when we question God, yet entropy persists. If our theology is unable to accommodate the reality of a loving, all-powerful God along with the reality of entropy, we will forever battle the temptation to drive a wedge between God and our lives. We may find ourselves questioning God's love. We may suppose bad things happen because God isn't all-loving. Or, we may hold on to God's love but find ourselves questioning God's power. We may suppose bad things happen because God isn't all-powerful. Tragically, we may even question the nature of evil itself. We may suppose bad things are just another aspect of God's nature. No! Let me encourage you to fight those lies at every turn. Time and again, Biblical authors cling to the truth of God's love and God's power in the face of real evil, real pain, and real despair. Read the Psalms. In this life, God has revealed that he is all-loving and all-powerful. He has revealed that evil is real, without fully answering the question of why or how long evil will run its course.

Please hear me, we are captives of entropy but only in part and only for a season. God has given us (here and now!) a foretaste of the life to come, the resurrection life where the tyranny of entropy will be swallowed up by life incorruptible. We are citizens of heaven (Phil. 3:20) by the resurrection of Christ. When we pledge our faithful allegiance to Jesus as the world's true Lord, we begin to experience (here and now!) eternal life. By the power of the resurrection we can go from bad to good, from death to life. We can reverse entropy every time (2Cor. 4:16).

As Christians, we fervently believe that spiritual renewal is a foretaste of the coming physical resurrection (1Cor. 15:23). In this world of disorder, the one sure thing is that entropy will run its course. We will grow old and die. But spiritually, we have already begun to experience the life of the world to come, the world where entropy and death are no more (1Cor. 15:24-26). Physically, everything goes downhill, from good to worse. But spiritually, by the power of the resurrection we can go from death to life, from sin to righteousness. It never fails. In a corruptible and sin-stained world we can already begin to experience the life of heaven, the life brought by the power of the resurrection.

Gentlemen, the pursuit of accomplishment often triggers our spiritual struggles. The allure of accomplishment grips us. We're visually oriented. We deal from the external. Life is often a race to climb the ladder, to scale the mountain, or to fill our treasure chest. We labor and slave to build an impressive tower of stuff. Stuff, sometimes fancy stuff but stuff nonetheless, can be the essence of our accomplishment. We remind ourselves that we are successful because of our house(s), our car(s), and our plasma screen(s). This whole mentality is nicely expressed by an old bumper sticker, "He who dies with the most toys wins." We do well to remember the counterpoint, "He who dies with the most toys is still dead." Every pile of stuff is a perishable crown, a temporary victory at best. Stuff grows old, accomplishments fade, and people die. These are truths that we know in our bones, yet you would hardly guess as much by the way we order our lives.

Sometimes the most profound truths are the most ignored because we assume that we've already dealt with them. We go on living as if entropy was a distant fairy tale and then find ourselves utterly deflated when it inevitably creeps up on us. I find the story of Job a wonderful corrective to this shortsighted tendency.

Job may very well be the oldest story in the Bible. Obviously, the events narrated in Genesis, "In the beginning," predate Job but the most ancient piece of literature in the canon of Scripture appears to be Job. It's an amazing story about a man who seemed utterly secure in his accomplishments. We are introduced to Job in the land of Uz. He is extremely wealthy. He has an abundance of children, livestock, houses and lands.

One day, the heavenly council gathers before God's throne. Satan (literally, the accuser) joins the gathering. God asks, "What ya' been doing?" Satan replies, "I've been patrolling the earth." God says, "Have you considered my man Job? He's spotless." Satan replies, "No wonder he loves you, he's got everything he could possibly want! On top of that you've protected him. If you but stretch out your hand against him he will curse you to your face." God says, "Go ahead. You can touch his stuff, just don't touch his body." Instantly, Job loses livestock, servants, houses, and children. He suffers incredible loss, but he does not curse God.

The story shifts back to the heavenly council. Satan returns. God asks, "What do you think of my man Job?" Satan answers, "Stuff is stuff, but his body is another thing altogether." Again, God grants permission: "Touch his body, but spare his life." Instantly, Job is afflicted with loathsome sores. He is left sitting on an ash heap, scraping boils with a shard of pottery. Can you imagine?! His wife pleads with him, "Curse God and die." More than a rebuke, I honestly think that she is pleading for Job to surrender. They have both been utterly devastated. Why not end the pain? What does Job have left?

Well, he has three friends. They show up and sit down next to him. For seven days they simply share his grief in silence. Then, they open their mouths. Unfortunately they aren't the most encouraging lot. They start saying things like, "Job, I'm not sure what it is but you must have done something pretty bad." Job probably wishes they would just shut-up and sit quietly again. Finally, Job cries out, "Why, God!?" God's reply is frighteningly direct, "Where were you, Job, when I hung out the world? Where were you when I drew the line between land and sea? Where were you, Job?" Job doesn't get a direct answer to the question *why*. Instead, he gets an answer in the form of *who*; specifically who he is in relation to Creator God.

Sometimes our passion dies because we don't get the kind of answers that we're searching for. We want different answers than God is offering. We want to know why our accomplishments wane and our possessions spoil. We want specific answers. We used to leap tall buildings in a single bound. These days, we can't even climb the corporate ladder without tripping all over ourselves. We ask, "Why, God!?" And the deafening silence begins to consume our passion. We face the battle of Job and we struggle to see our way through. Spiritual battle is profoundly difficult. When the question *why* has no good answer, what will sustain us? The very same thing that sustained Job, the person, the *who*, of Creator God. The answer is more relational than doctrinal. Like Job, we will never in this life know all of the *whys*, but we can know the Person who remains with us through the trials of life. It is this Person, rather than abstract doctrine, who saved Job and restored the blessings of children, land, and possessions at the end of the story. Yet even then, Job never knew why he faced the battle.

Guys, the battles of life will confront us at the very core of our being. They will challenge our most fundamental concepts of meaning and identity. Our crown of accomplishments will perpetually be withering under the force of entropy. If our driving force is simply a matter of emotional energy, we will spend our entire lives trying to stir up the emotional cauldron. We will forever be searching for the magic elixir that sparks our engine. If our motivation is nothing more than emotional excitement, our life's work will be a halting series of exaggerated ups and downs, a rollercoaster of cosmic proportions. We can spend our lives searching for the next emotional fix, or we can learn to lash our lives to a different vessel. We can anchor ourselves to something more stable than the emotional whims of the moment.

Instead of manipulating emotional experience, we can commit to character development. Emotions are glorious gifts that add color and vibrancy to life's experience. However, we are to become stewards of our emotions, not captives. Emotions are not to be the rudder of our life's journey. There is a better way to be human. That way is defined by determination more than emotion. The essence of determination is a stable choice. Determination is a choice that says, "Just one more day, one more time, I will choose to seek God's will. Just one more day, one more time, I will choose to follow God's way." Such determination will carry us through the ebbs and flows of emotional fervor.

Determination is a choice, not an emotion. Something will replace emotional passion when it wanes. In the absence of determination, other contenders will jockey for position. More often than not, the winning contender is a posture of grumbling. When emotions wane and determination is absent, we become grumblers. We become people who find the worst in every situation. Before long, we find ourselves trapped in a downward spiral from which we see no light, "Things could be worse, and sure enough they will be!" Grumbling.

I love the Old Testament. It crackles with the drama of life. It is visual. It is visceral. Throughout the Old Testament, the story of Israel is the stage for God's work in the world. The story of Israel is replete with passion and grumbling. Consider the Exodus story. The people of Israel have been slaves in Egypt for hundreds of years. Moses, their God-appointed leader, returns from hiding in the wilderness to demand their freedom, "Let my people go!" Pharaoh says, "Fat chance." A duel ensues between the God of Israel and the gods of Egypt. The gods of Egypt, the land of Egypt, and the people of Egypt are utterly decimated by a series of plagues, from the river of blood to the angel of death. Pharaoh is moved from obstinate resistance to shattered pleading. He begs Moses, "Get out of here! You and your people!" The Israelites leave in haste and Egypt literally gives them the wealth of the land.

In the drama of the moment, the nation of Israel begins a long march into the unknown. They find themselves moving toward an apparent dead end with walls on either side and the Red Sea in front of them. They turn and realize, "Oh, no! Here comes Pharaoh's army! We're dead! Moses you idiot, why did you bring us out here to die?!" God commands Moses to stretch out his staff. Imagine as the waters of the Red Sea roll back and they walk through the depths of the sea on a highway in the wilderness. How utterly surreal. I'm sure that all the little boys just couldn't help themselves from poking their fingers into the walls of water. I'm also sure that every mother shouted, "Be careful! Don't do that!"

When they get to the other side they look and see Pharaoh's army in hot pursuit. "Oh, no! Moses, pull back the walls of water!" God's Spirit moves over the waters and Pharaoh's army is suddenly bobbing like apples in the middle of the Red Sea. The Israelites have a party. Miriam breaks into song. The people sing and dance and continue their march into the unknown. They head toward the Promised Land, by way of the wilderness.

Three days later they arrive at an oasis. They need water, but the oasis is bitter. "Moses! You idiot! What are we going to drink? Why did you bring us out here to die?!" Moses cries out to God. God shows him a piece of wood. Moses throws it into the water and the water becomes sweet (what a wonderful picture). They leave the oasis and travel further into the wilderness. "Moses, you idiot! You brought us out here and we don't have any food. If we eat our cattle we won't have any breed stock. If we eat our seed, we won't have anything to plant. Our kids are dying. Back in Egypt we could at least sit by our pots and eat bread. We're dying out here!" God speaks to Moses, "If it's bread they want, then bread they'll get. I have some amazing stuff up here. I'll throw it from the sky each morning and everyone can eat their fill." The people called the bread manna (literally, "what's this?"). As promised, the manna was amazing. You could bake it. You could boil it. You could slice it. You could dice it. It was great stuff. The only catch was that manna had a shelf-life of twenty-four hours (on Friday that shelf-life doubled to forty-eight hours so they could observe the Sabbath rest). Manna was incredible. It was free, for nothing. What more could the people want? Plenty.

After they leave Mt. Sinai with God's Law in hand, the people start grumbling—again! You could hear the tin cups rattling all over camp, "We want meat! We want meat! We used to have fish, melons, and leeks in the land of Egypt. Now, our strength is dried up and we have nothing to look at but this paltry manna. We want meat!" Moses is at his wit's end. "God, did I give birth to this people that I should carry them like a mother? Where can I possibly get enough meat to feed these cry-babies?" At this point, God has had quite enough himself. "They want meat? I'll give them meat until it pours out of their nostrils!" Moses makes the mistake of questioning God's sincerity, and receives an answer very similar to Job's: "Is the Lord's power limited?" (Num. 11:23).

It's not good to get God upset. He causes a wind to blow a few quail into the camp. Quail covered the ground for a distance of fifteen to twenty miles (a day's walk) in any direction. Not only that, the quail were stacked at least three feet deep. There were feathers as far as the eye could see. The people worked night and day gathering quail. Their baskets were running over. "But while the meat was still between their teeth, before it was consumed, the anger of the Lord was kindled against the people, and the Lord struck the people with a very great plague," (Num. 11:33). Suddenly, it was the bodies of dead Israelites that covered the ground as far as the eye could see. Grumbling was their undoing.

Without determination, grumbling becomes our undoing. Without determination grumbling, griping, and selfish questioning bubble to the surface, "Why me?! Why is my life so much harder than it used to be? Why is my life so much harder than other people I know? What am I, chopped liver?" We grumble. We neither see nor remember how God has cared for us. A long memory is absolutely critical for a healthy faith. A short memory is a recipe for grumbling and discontent. The nation of ancient Israel is a perfect example.

The Lord sustained an entire nation in the middle of the wilderness (for forty years!) and they couldn't see it. Their provision was as regular as clockwork, yet they grumbled. Looking back, we may excuse their grumbling. I mean after all, they were wandering in the wilderness. However if that's how we feel, then our situation should absolutely preclude grumbling. We Americans live in the wealthiest, most affluent nation in the history of the world. I am not exaggerating. If you've read anything of history, if you've looked at anything in this world today, then you realize that we live in an immensely powerful and prosperous culture. Yet, we grumble. No matter what our context or culture, if our passion isn't fortified with determination, we'll grumble. I am challenged by that awareness because I struggle with grumbling just as much as anyone else.

I am always humbled and encouraged by the opening events of Luke's Gospel. What an amazing story. Here is a couple, Zechariah and Elizabeth, immortalized in Scripture as righteous and blameless (Luke 1:6). What a wonderful legacy, righteous and blameless. But, they had no children. That was a serious problem. It was also shocking. In one verse, Luke writes that Zechariah and Elizabeth were righteous. In the very next verse, he indicates their barrenness. That just doesn't add up! How could a righteous couple be barren? It was an utter contradiction in terms (almost as bad as a crucified Messiah!). In ancient Israel, as in many ancient cultures, barrenness was interpreted as divine displeasure. Barrenness meant that something was wrong. Yet, Luke would have us believe that Zechariah and Elizabeth were not only righteous and blameless, they were also members of the priestly order. Elizabeth was a descendent of Aaron and Zechariah belonged to the priestly class of Abijah. My goodness! But wait, there's more. Before diving into the narrative Luke heightens the tension by telling us that Zechariah and Elizabeth were both getting old…

Zechariah went to Jerusalem for his days of service at the Temple. This would have been a special but regular business trip. Put simply, there were more priests than slots of service at the Temple. So, they worked in shifts. During the shift of the priests of Abijah, Zechariah would have helped with the regular Temple liturgy. However, something extraordinary happened on this trip. It began when Zechariah was chosen by lot to offer incense in the sanctuary of the Lord. Some priests would serve their entire lives without being chosen for this privilege, but Zechariah had his day! Can you imagine the emotional passion, the intensity? He was probably thinking, "I'm gonna have my shot! I'm gonna have my chance!" And Liz probably kept saying, "Zach, just enjoy it. You'll do well."

Finally, his morning came. He entered the sanctuary and could hardly contain himself. I'm sure his heart was pounding when he entered the Holy place. He would have gawked. He was finally there. Then, the training would have kicked in and he would have started to perform his service unto Yahweh.

All of a sudden, the hair on the back of his neck began to tingle. A palpable presence had joined him in the Holy place. This wasn't extemporaneous worship. There wasn't supposed to be anyone there. He turned around and nearly hyperventilated. To the right of the altar stood a really big angel. The angel said, "Fear not," (yeah, right). "Zechariah, your prayer has been heard. Your wife Elizabeth will bear a son, and you shall name him John. He will make ready a people prepared for the Lord."

I don't know if angels take breaths, but when this angel finally paused for a moment Zechariah blurted out, "How can this be!? I'm an old man. My wife's an old woman. How can this happen?" Big mistake. The angel ruffled his feathers. "I'm Gabriel. I've come from the presence of God. Because you don't believe my words...I'm going to shrink you down until you're only two feet tall." Is that what the angel said? Or, "I'm going to shrivel your arms so it looks like you've got chicken wings." Is that what Gabriel said? No. He said, "You will become mute, unable to speak, until the day these things occur."

I believe that Zechariah's speechlessness was a purposeful sign. It was more than a random inconvenience. Think with me for a moment. What unique, creative ability has God given humanity? Speech. Have you ever considered the wonder of human speech? An idea occurs in your brain. A few nerves spark. Your diaphragm contracts and expels air through your bronchial tubes. The air moves across your tongue, teeth, and lips. That air carries sound waves outside your body. Those sound waves excite molecules that move across the intervening space and hit the side of someone's head. The sound travels down a small tube (if there's not too much ear wax) and excite a little piece of skin. Three little bones twitch and excite some nerves inside the brain. All of this occurs in a mere instant and the other person's brain deciphers the sound. Your thought is translated into someone else's understanding. Talk about creativity! We can even nuance our speech so the same little sound ("ah") indicates pleasure ("Ah! That was a great meal!") or pain ("Ah! That coffee is hot!"). Isn't it amazing? God removed Zechariah's most creative capacity, aside from procreation, to indicate quite clearly that God Himself was the source of creation. Elizabeth's pregnancy was not to be understood as a random biological quirk. This pregnancy was the active involvement of Creator God.

When Zechariah finally came out of the Temple, the people were all jittery. "What's going on? We thought you might have dropped dead!" All Zechariah could do was flail and motion. The people responded, "What's this?! He can't talk, and his behavior is really weird. Liz, take the poor boy home before he flips out." Elizabeth took him home. She comforted him. She became pregnant and gave birth nine months later. On the eighth day they took the baby to the Temple to circumcise, to dedicate, and to name. Everyone was so happy for the old couple. "Ah Liz, how wonderful! You've had a Zach, Jr." Elizabeth replies, "Actually, we're going to name him John." They say, "But you don't have any John's in your family." This prompts more mumbling from Zach. They say, "Well, let's check. Give him something to write with. Let's find out for sure."

I like to think that as soon as Zechariah wrote that first letter he burst out with a loud voice, "JOHN! We're naming this baby, John. And by the way I did see an angel, you idiots!" This John, the Baptist, was the forerunner of the Christ. He must have been one of the most intense, determined dudes chronicled in the pages of Scripture. He wore camel hair and ate bugs for goodness sake. This guy was intense. He even confronted King Herod, and paid with his life. I like to think that John learned about the finer points of determination from his father, Zechariah, the priest who discovered the key to determined trust. When John was about knee-high, Zechariah may have sat him down and said, "John, if an angel ever shows up, just do it!" Just one more day, just one more time, do it God's way. A determined father taught a son who became the forerunner of the Christ. Yes, he had questions. Yes, he had doubts (Matt. 11:3). However, his determination made him a successful messenger. He turned the hearts of his people to their Lord.

7

PASSION IN WOMEN:
COMMITMENT WITH PURPOSE

And there was a prophetess, Anna the daughter of Phanuel, of the tribe of Asher. She was advanced in years, having lived with a husband seven years after her marriage, and then as a widow to the age of eighty-four. And she never left the temple, serving night and day with fastings and prayers. And at that very moment she came up, and began giving thanks to God, and continued to speak of Him to all those who were looking for the redemption of Jerusalem.

~ Luke 2:36-38

From Elaine:

After my daughter died, I found myself living in a very masculine home. My husband and two teenage sons were all very masculine and very passionate about sports—especially football. I was not. Much to their surprise, I didn't enjoy scheduling our family meals around kickoff or halftime of a televised football game. When our meals started feeling like halftime entertainment, I actually offered to put dinner in a blender so they could just suck it up and get back to the TV. Thankfully it never came to that, but I began to sense a growing passion for family activities that we could all enjoy. By the time Christmas rolled around, I felt a burning passion to make the Holiday special. As we continued working through our individual and corporate grieving, I was determined to create new traditions and pursue a life of hope.

When our sons decided they wanted to enjoy the thrill of downhill skiing, I took the plunge and booked family reservations. The boys were thrilled. I was terrified. As I mentioned earlier, I am not passionate about sports. I do not consider myself athletic. At the time, I was also forty years old and, unlike the boys, I did not have a need for speed. I was a bit nervous so I decided to schedule a private lesson my first day on the slopes. My young instructor was very patient and very clear. Everything he taught and demonstrated made perfect sense in my head. The problem came when I actually had to move my body. I was literally scared stiff. My instructor actually had to ski backwards and pull the tips of my skis to get me moving. He kept saying, "You have to move to turn."

As I quickly learned, a commitment to skiing requires a commitment to speed and force. It's simply not possible to make good turns, let alone come to a stop, unless you generate speed and apply force. Since I was unwilling to embrace either speed or force, I discovered that falling was an effective alternative. Snow drifts were a wonderful resource. The trick was finding a snow drift big enough to cushion my fall but small enough so I could actually get back up. I did eventually learn to enjoy skiing, but only after I approached it with a measure of passion—doing whatever it took to make it down the mountain.

Passion. We have considered passion as intense emotion and desire. As I indicated in the previous chapter, and as Elaine just illustrated in her story about learning to ski, so little seems to happen without some sort of emotional excitement. A passionate person can accomplish much. Because of this we find ourselves constantly searching for additional passion, expending incredible amounts of energy to conjure and sustain a momentary sensation. Passion is a wonderful thing, but it won't last forever. Entropy will have its day. Situations change, we grow old, and passion wanes. We lose our edge. We read about the martyrs and wonder, "Could I sacrifice that much for the Kingdom? What kind of passion would it take?"

In a broken world of trouble and strife, passion must be built with purpose. Our purpose finds meaning in the resurrection of Jesus Christ. Entropy persists, but our hope is grounded in the future light that has broken into this present darkness (2Cor. 4:16). There is a better way to be human, the way of sacrificial love, stewardship, and forgiveness. Without carefully directed meaning, we will find ourselves trapped in a cycle of grumbling when passion inevitably wanes.

My first class in college was astronomy. The professor was utterly passionate about the subject. His passion was contagious. More than forty years later, I still love astronomy. I'm not sure what ever happened to that professor, but I hope he lived long enough to see at least the first images captured by the Hubble Space Telescope. To see those pictures and to know that our Heavenly Father spoke this universe into existence is an utterly humbling and awe-inspiring experience. We live next to a little star that we call our sun. Astronomically speaking, it's a rather average G-class star. Astronomically speaking, there is nothing particularly outstanding or noteworthy about our sun. For our purpose the truly remarkable thing is that planet earth is positioned just the right distance from our sun to facilitate carbon-based life. We are situated a comfortable 93 million miles away, which makes our planet neither too hot nor too cold. To quote Goldilocks, the conditions on planet earth are "just right."

Our distance of 93 million miles translates into about eight light-minutes. Light travels at the speed of roughly 186,000 miles per second. So, from the time light emanates from the sun, it takes approximately eight minutes to reach us. If the sun winked out, we wouldn't know it for eight minutes. The next closest star to our planet is the Dog Star. The Dog Star is located 3.4 light years away. In other words it takes light almost three-and-a-half years, traveling at 186,000 miles per second, to get here. That's a long way! It makes you wonder if God was worried that we'd mess up the neighborhood. Our solar system is situated in the corner of a galaxy called the Milky Way. Our galaxy contains 160-175 million stars. In the middle of the summer, on a really clear night, you can literally peer through the stars of our galaxy—millions of them. The next closest galaxy is called Andromeda. It's a spiral nebula containing between 175-200 million stars. Andromeda is 100,000 light years away. That's a ridiculously long way!

With the Hubble telescope and radio telescopes we can peer to the far reaches of the universe and detect the effects of a big bang "in the beginning." The further we peer, the less defined galaxies appear because we are literally looking back in time. The light that we see is 8-10 billion years old. Put simply, that light is seriously old news. Because of this time lag, we haven't seen these galaxies develop into spiral nebulas under the force of gravity. Nevertheless it seems pretty clear that these galaxies are actually larger and more dense than our own. The last I heard, astronomers project 800 million to 1 billion galaxies with an average of 300-400 million stars each. The size and scope of the universe is utterly mind-boggling.

I include this astronomical survey for a specific reason. In a world with billions of people and a universe with billions upon billions of stars, we can each feel pretty small. Yet God calls each and every star by name and knows their numbers (Psa. 147:4). Not only that, He knows each and every person. In the book of Jeremiah we hear God tell the Babylonian exiles, "I will listen to you" (Jer. 29:12). Reinforcing this message in the New Testament, Matthew's Gospel promises that Christ will be with us to the very end of the age (Matt. 28:20). Don't ever forget these promises. Don't ever let the voice of a tempter crowd them out. In the midst of our daily struggles, questions may bubble to the surface. Voices may whisper in our ear, "God can't hear you. Think about it, almost 7 billion people live on this planet. You're about as significant as a pebble." Don't buy that line for a second. The infinite Creator God will never be distracted by numbers. He knows you by name and cares for you, personally (Psa. 139:1-18).

"And I will listen to you." Ladies, when you are listened to (i.e., respected) you may find your passion growing. Attention can generate passion. On the other hand, when no one seems to care and you feel reduced to nothing, passion withers and dies. "I will listen to you." Being listened to is closely related to being loved. However, being listened to and being loved don't guarantee smooth sailing in life. When the difficult times come, firm commitment and a clear purpose often make the difference between victory or defeat, passion or depression. Define your purpose through prayer and the study of God's Word. Scripture is light and truth. It is worthy of our obedience and passion. When your intercessory prayers are humble, passionate, and purposeful, they can touch the very heart of God. Combined with insight and awareness, such prayers are a powerful force. Remember, God promises to listen. Elaine and I consistently prayed that our sons would grow up to be mighty, Godly men in spirit and in truth. To this end, we applied discipline in practical ways. Our children have now left home but I can still remember their childhood days of schoolwork and exams. On certain days, like the day before a test, you could almost sense something palpable in the air. Early in the evening my wife and I would pick up a low-level buzz circulating between the kids. Before long the truth would leak out: one of them had a test the next day. With this knowledge in hand, we would casually watch for any significant changes in study habits that night. Regardless of any study changes, the real drama always happened the next morning, the morning of the test. Once or twice the morning of the test began with a shocking announcement, "Oh, dad I got a really bad gut-ache. I don't think I can go to school today." My reply, "Oh, really? Don't you have a test today?" The writhing response, "Yeah, but my gut really hurts dad."

"Get up."

"Oh, dad!"

"Get up."

"But, dad!"

"Did you study last night?"

"Well…"

"Get up."

"Dad, why are you so mean?"

"Because when you're forty-five years old I don't want you still living in my house. Get up and get an education so you can go get a job."

Now, don't you think that God loves us at least that much? I do. Despite the billions of dollars that we spend on the entertainment industry, the most important question in this life is not, "What do I enjoy?" The most important question is, "How can I be of use to God?" In other words, the greatest issue of life has more to do with mission than emotion. Mission is our purpose. It is true in this life and it will continue to be true in the life to come. Our effectiveness in God's Kingdom (now and then) is not primarily a function of our emotional energy. Our effectiveness is mostly a matter of persistent obedience. In our culture of entertainment and emotional satisfaction, it is especially important for us to shape and discipline our desires. As Christians, we dare not assume that all of our desires must be God-given and therefore indulged. Appetites can be learned. Evil is real. "The heart is devious above all else," (Jer. 17:9). If we believe that this life is a prelude for an even greater life to come, then we have every reason to be serious about character formation here-and-now. Our service to God in the future will be a function of our character in the present. In other words, we are best prepared for eternity when we learn to serve God in the limits of the present. We are most valuable to the Kingdom as we learn to grow in the wisdom of a crucified Savior. Only then are we truly fitted for resurrection life.

Please don't misunderstand what I am saying. Intercessory prayer is a healthy response to pain and struggle. We literally groan for redemption (Rom. 8). Yet, these prayers are actually intercessions for God's future (the final defeat of evil) to make itself known in the present (where evil still does harm). We are praying for God's Kingdom to come, "on earth as it is in Heaven." Until God's Kingdom arrives in a full manifestation of power and glory, we can expect our determined obedience and purposeful commitment to be the clearest witnesses to God's Kingdom in the present. Furthermore, our obedience actually embodies and incarnates God's Kingdom in this world. In the midst of our trials, we are not only to intercede for relief (i.e., for the coming of God's Kingdom) but we are also to view our trials as potential bearers of God's Kingdom in our lives. Our purposeful commitment now announces God's Kingdom and testifies to His divine love that will flood the world to come.

In the absence of purposeful commitment and faithfulness, we may find ourselves lapsing into the grumbling we explored in the previous chapter. Another possible response is stubborn self-sufficiency, a form of manipulation. A self-sufficient resolve doesn't grumble and complain to God. In fact, it doesn't acknowledge Him at all. The manipulative woman says, "I'll just take care of this situation myself." The spiritual Lone Ranger cuts God out of the picture altogether. The problem with this mentality has nothing to do with individual ability. It's not that some people, be they male or female, young or old, are more capable than others. The issue is not ability but trust. Spiritually speaking, the most destructive attitude is the one that says, "I won't trust. I've been hurt one too many times and I'm just going to keep my trust to myself." The point is not that we trust people because we think they are trustworthy. The point is that we trust people because we believe that God is trustworthy. Our trust is our proclamation that God is finally and ultimately faithful even if other people let us down (as they surely will). I am not encouraging naivety or blind foolishness, but I am exhorting Christians to self-giving and sacrificial love. Our trust in others ultimately reveals our trust in the Lord.

The way you trust those around you illustrates how you trust the Lord. This type of thinking is what lies behind a passage like 1 Peter 3:1:

> You wives, be submissive to your own husbands so that even if any of them are disobedient to the word, they may be won without a word by the behavior of their wives.

In similar fashion, Paul encourages wives to be submissive to their husbands "as to the Lord," (Eph. 5:22). Please understand something. You never demonstrate trust just so others can see and take note. You demonstrate trust for your own benefit as well. When you are committed to trust God in the circumstances of your life, you foster a seedbed for spiritual vitality and determined character. In practice, you come to know that you can intercede and that God hears you. This is difficult and wrenching work, but it is the very work that transforms our trials into vehicles of grace. In the midst of betrayal and pain, trust is our testimony rather than our weakness.

This may not be the most politically correct statement but I believe that it is just as difficult for women to trust as it is for men to love. Husbands are commanded to love their wives just as (i.e., equal to) the way Christ loved those under his authority. Whenever men assume leadership positions they are required to choose for the highest good of those under their authority. Consider just how difficult that is for your average male (i.e., ego-maniac). His top concern is probably more along the lines of, "I! Me!" By contrast, women seem to love with relative ease. Have you ever noticed how any woman within eyesight of a newborn just coos and coddles, no matter what the infant looks like? "Oh, isn't this just the most beautiful baby!" Never mind that the poor child just endured a grueling thirty-five hour birthing process. Never mind that it's all red and hairy and beat-up with a cone-shaped head. The new father takes one look at the newborn and says, "Dear God! Do you think it will ever grow out of that?" Meanwhile momma and all the women just coo and coddle. Dad is thinking, "My child looks like hamburger!"

My point is that men typically must learn to love. It might happen quickly, perhaps the second time a father holds his newborn, but it's still a learning process. Ladies usually experience love as a more innate tendency. It's the easiest thing in the world for a nurturing person to love. However, it's a different matter altogether when it comes to trust. Trust is a more precarious and threatening endeavor because personal security is on the line. It requires passion and purposeful commitment. Suppose a lady can see right through some guy. He's as transparent as a pane of glass. The most natural response will not be trust. It will probably be more along the lines of, "Why in the world should I trust him?!" Yet this is the very point where committed trust serves witness. In a broken and cynical world, passionately committed trust proclaims that God is ultimately faithful, even when others let us down.

There's an amazing little story in the second chapter of Luke. It occurs shortly after the account of Elizabeth, Zechariah, and the birth of John the Baptist. Six months after John's birth, Jesus the Messiah is born. On the eighth day, Mary and Joseph take their baby to the Temple to dedicate, to circumcise, and to name. As they come into the Temple, Luke mentions two additional characters. First, there was a man named Simeon. Simeon, "was righteous and devout, looking for the consolation of Israel," (Luke 2:25). "There was [also] a prophetess, Anna the daughter of Phanuel, of the tribe of Asher. She was advanced in years, having lived with a husband seven years after her marriage, and then as a widow to the age of eighty-four," (Luke 2:36-37).

I love this story. Luke is a marvelous storyteller. Sandwiched within his account of the Holy Family, we are given a small yet sharp window into the lives of Simeon and Anna, two faithful saints. Both are advanced in years. Both are people of passion and purpose. They are the kind of people who inspire by their lives. Perhaps this is why Luke chose to include them in his narrative. Other storytellers and artists have followed his lead.

My wife and I visited the Louvre during one of our teaching trips to Europe. We were awed by the monstrous rooms, the vaulted ceilings, and the enormous Renaissance paintings. I remember walking into one particular room because we wanted to see a specific painting. Despite being ignorant tourists, we knew right where it was when we saw the sea of people. Making our way through the crowd, we walked up to it and were surprised to hear several people say, "But it's so small." As you may have figured out, the painting was the *Mona Lisa*. Given the popularity and stature of this work, we were rather surprised to see just how small it actually was. It amounted to one little (though impressive) work of art on one little space of wall. The contrast was all the more striking because it was surrounded by several larger paintings. One of these surrounding images was called *The Dedication*. It depicted a mother holding her baby. As you can imagine, this was no ordinary mother and no ordinary child. A halo adorned the mother's head and a prominent shaft of light illuminated the babe. Other notable figures included a glassy-eyed father and a venerable old man administering a blessing. I'm no art historian but the work struck me as an altogether typical Renaissance picture of Mary, Joseph, and Jesus. From my perspective, the truly remarkable element was the gnarled old lady beaming in the background. It was the prophetess Anna.

She had lived with her husband for seven years. As we have discussed in earlier chapters, childbearing in ancient Israel, as in many cultures, was both an honor and a duty. In the ancient world societies depended on high fertility rates for their very survival. Because of this, most women married as soon as they reached child-bearing age. Anna probably got married somewhere between the age of twelve and fifteen. At the same time, most righteous men of Israel married at the age of thirty. This was considered the age of male maturity. Now here's the catch. Male life-expectancy was roughly thirty-six to thirty-eight years. Men would be married for six to eight years, and then they'd die. Let's just assume that Anna married when she was thirteen and lived with her husband for seven years. That would have made her twenty years old when he died at the ripe old age of thirty-seven. Now, what was she going to do? It was not a pretty picture. Yes, the Jewish law of posterity obliged her husband's closest brother to provide a child for the dead man's legacy (Deut. 25:5-10). However, we only have to read the story of Ruth to realize that economics sometimes got in the way of that little provision (Ruth 4:6). The care of widows was a perpetual social problem in the ancient world. Paul even addressed the issue when writing to Timothy (1Tim. 5). These widows were not necessarily old ladies. They included teenagers and twenty-year-olds. So there was Anna, the widow. She was one of a multitude of widows.

"And she never left the temple, serving night and day with fastings and prayers," (Luke 2:37). A twenty-year-old widow goes to the Temple and dedicates herself to fasting and prayer for the next sixty-four years. That's intense. That's passion. That's commitment with a purpose. She committed herself to the temple for sixty-four years. "And at that very moment she came up and began giving thanks to God, and continued to speak of Him to all those who were looking for the redemption of Jerusalem," (Luke 2:38). What an amazing incident. The Temple was not some cozy little spot where it was easy to find people. It would be a mistake for us to pretend it was some quaint little gathering. The Jerusalem Temple was monstrous. It was like a mega-church, a market, and city hall all rolled into one. Thousands of people packed the Temple courts every day. At the height of the sacrificial calendar, up to thirty-thousand animals were killed on a single day in preparation for Passover.

The Temple was a messy, intense, money-changing place. At this point in her life, Anna was a gnarled eighty-four year old widow shuffling her way through the jostling buzz and bustle of Temple life. As Luke would have us believe, she happened upon Simeon with a young family and—*bam!*—the Holy Spirit affirmed her deepest prayer, "This child is the one." I seriously doubt that a shaft of light spanned the heavens and illuminated the Babe. I suspect that Mary's head looked quite normal and no halo was perched atop her brow. Nevertheless, Anna saw him and she knew. She saw him, the one whom she had prayed about for sixty-four years, never leaving the Temple in fasting and prayer for the redemption of Jerusalem. Isn't God good? She labored in prayer for sixty-four years, and Holy Scripture contains the fulfillment of her passionate and purposeful commitment. Passion.

If the prayers of one woman can accomplish such results, imagine what can happen with a group of Spirit-filled women. I challenge you to pray with passion, and to be committed to God's purposes. Intercede with intensity and trust that God will change your world, be it now or be it years down the road. God will achieve His purposes and we have the privilege of cooperating in His work through passionate prayer and action. May God's listening love fuel your passion. May our churches pray with determined obedience and purposeful commitment until God's Kingdom comes on earth as it is in heaven.

8

THE FOCUS OF MAN:
THE NEED FOR RESPECT

And my God will supply all your needs according to His riches in glory in Christ Jesus.

~ *Philippians 4:19*

One of the great adventures of the 20th Century was the Apollo space program. The entire series of Apollo space missions represented an amazing feat. For the first time in recorded history, humans ventured past the bonds of earth and turned their attention to earth's closest neighbor, the moon. Early Apollo missions instilled a growing sense of confidence and possibility. By the time Apollo 13 rolled around, we were appropriately cautious but exceedingly confident. Self-assured human nature was gathering steam.

On April 13, 1970 the Apollo 13 astronauts were two days into their journey. They were thousands of miles away from planet earth and moving at a speed of more than 15,000 mph. Every moment of the mission was a technological marvel. Given the perilous nature of their mission, you might have thought the entire country would be on pins and needles. However, when the astronauts held a news conference from the reaches of outer space, the major television networks didn't even provide coverage. Granted, there were no twenty-four hour news stations at the time, but the broadcast decision was still telling. Most Americans had become blasé.

After the unheralded news conference the astronauts did some basic housekeeping chores and prepared for their sleep cycle. The following day was going to be a big one. They were scheduled to enter the moon's orbit. Before bedding down, one of the astronauts flipped a switch. All of a sudden sirens blared and the capsule began to gyrate. Sensors indicated that oxygen levels were dropping. Not only that, an electric generator failed and they had to shut it down. The entire mission was instantly compromised. They would no longer be able to land on the moon. More pressing still, life support systems were jeopardized. The situation was growing desperate. In the span of a few short breaths, that small capsule was transformed from confident optimism to frustration, fear, and anger. What was going on? One of the astronauts radioed back to earth, "Houston, we have a problem."

They had a problem all right. Can you imagine? They were two hundred thousand miles away from Earth. They couldn't exactly pull over and stop at a spaceship warehouse to pick up spare parts. Not only that, they were moving away from their only source of help at a rate of 15,000 mph! The very possibility of getting home took on a whole new urgency. They faced the daunting prospect of circling around the moon and firing their rockets for a return journey, unsure if they would even have sufficient electricity or oxygen to make it home. The astronauts of Apollo 13 went from a frustrating problem (a scrubbed mission) to a desperate need (resources for the journey home).

We tend to interchange these two words pretty easily—problem and need. We tend to think of them as quite similar. However, there is a significant difference between the two. I can usually solve problems by myself, but needs make me dependent. A problem is something that I can usually solve if I apply sufficient time, talent, energy, and resources. I might not want to deal with my problem but if I apply myself I can probably solve it. A need is something different. A need is something that I cannot take care of myself. A need cannot be solved by applying personal time, talent, energy, and resources. The astronauts of Apollo 13 needed hundreds of engineers working thousands of man hours assembling models and testing hypothetical solutions. Their salvation required the ingenuity and assistance of others. Without a support team, the astronauts of Apollo 13 would simply have spun off into, "Infinity and Beyond!" The astronauts had a need. They had a desperate need. No matter how much time and personal energy they applied, they could never have met this need on their own.

In our waking and working hours, it is all too easy to focus on the problems in our lives. It's easy to develop a shortsighted tendency that artificially shrinks our perspective to personal problems. Whether we find ourselves hurtling toward the dark side of the moon or in the more familiar reaches of a grocery store, I want to suggest that focusing on personal problems is the wrong place to direct our spiritual energy. When problems become our focus we tend to overlook larger issues, even critical issues. Imagine what would have happened if the Apollo 13 astronauts failed to repair their capsule because they were so dejected about a scrubbed mission. It may seem hard to imagine, but we make the same mistake in principle when physical, emotional, or spiritual problems become the sole objects of our attention. We overlook larger issues. We fail to find peace. You see, problems never end. Before long we start to feel like a postal worker during the holidays: the mail never stops coming! When our focus is trained on a perpetual stream of daily problems, the result is unending turmoil.

Rain or shine, we know that we're going to face problems in this life. You might wake up in the morning thinking that everything is swell, until you suddenly realize that you misplaced your keys. "Where are they?!" That's a problem. Now, if you apply enough time, talent, energy, and resources you will probably find your keys. You know they're somewhere in the house. You just don't know which pile of stuff they're hiding under. This is a small example but it makes the point. Every single day we face problems. Problems are a normal part of life.

Not only are problems maddeningly relentless, they are also frustratingly unfair. We always seem to be the ones who end up with the fuzzy end of the lollipop. Everybody else seems to get a break. "What am I, chopped liver?!" It seems so unfair. In fact, that may be the case. Fairness is a good liberal modern concept. God is more concerned with justice than fairness. The fact is, human structures are flawed. This is true even (or maybe, especially) in the church. Things get missed. People fall through cracks. After a while, we can start to feel like the odds are stacked against us. Problems seem to grow exponentially, especially when we're alone. Before we know it, a small stack of problems has grown into a mountain of despair.

Isn't it interesting that God promises to supply all of our needs? Again, a need is something that we are not going to solve no matter how much time, talent, energy, or resources we apply. Sometimes we suffer physical pain and we want God to meet our problem. Sometimes God does heal physical pain but we do well to maintain a proper perspective. In my advanced stage of (late-middle) life, I have looked around and noticed that I don't see any 900 year-old people walking the surface of the earth. I'm sure you've noticed too. Thousands of years ago the psalmist faced the same reality, recognizing that we are given seventy years or eighty if by strength (Psa. 90:10). These days many people live past their eighties and into their nineties. In fact, centenarians represent one of the fastest growing demographics of our time. However as a percentage of overall population, centenarians are miniscule. Most people (still) reach their end of days somewhere between seventy and eighty years. I don't care how much you run. I don't care how many bean sprouts you eat. I don't care how much yogurt you consume. Somewhere between seventy and eighty—that's it. Human life is term-limited.

How might this reality affect our perception of physical problems? If we are suffering and the only thing we pray for is relief, what about the next time? And the time after that? And the next? If we're not careful we may actually paint ourselves into a corner where the life to come sounds like an inconvenient and unfortunate event. We may find ourselves wanting nothing more than the passing pleasure of this momentary life. Please remember, this life is temporary. We may not enjoy talking about death when we have so many trinkets and toys at our disposal, but that doesn't change the cold hard facts. Our lives are term-limited. Be thankful. I don't want this to be the best I ever experience. Do you?

God sees and knows all of our needs. He knows our thoughts before we think them. He has the hairs of our heads numbered (an easier job in my case). He understands and knows us. God is all-knowing and all-powerful. I believe in divine healing. I have witnessed physical, emotional, and spiritual healing in my own life and in the lives of others. I don't understand why God heals some people and not others but that question actually misses the point. The point is that this world is not my final home. There is a better, redeemed world yet to come. Heaven and earth will meet as one. Until that occurs, my need in this life is a proper perspective. I need a perspective that prepares me for the life to come. In the midst of frustration, suffering, and pain God has met and will continue to meet that need.

The Kingdom of Heaven is not a beauty pageant. Jesus made this point crystal clear when he said that it was better to cut off troublesome body parts than to be cut off from God's Kingdom (Matt. 5:29-30). God wants to teach us. We need to comprehend the life of the world to come. We need to know what it means to be fit for the life of eternity. That's where our need lies. Yes, God has provided gracious solutions to some of our physical problems but those are not the ultimate solutions. They are only provisional. When the Lord raised Lazarus from the dead the poor guy still faced the specter of mortal life and a second death (John 11). At best, physical healing is a signal pointing the way forward to God's coming Kingdom.

I am legally blind because of degenerative eye disease. If you are anything like me, blindness probably isn't on your list of life goals. It wasn't on my list either. In fact it utterly destroyed some of my life goals. Blindness is not something I want. I'm not thrilled about it. Many people have asked if they could publicly pray for my healing. I have usually agreed but it creates an interesting dynamic. Public prayer can take on the appearance of performance. If nothing happens then people start wondering if something is wrong with the prayer or the person being prayed for. Sometimes I even start to wonder if my faith is deficient. Unanswered prayer can generate unpleasant feelings but I have committed myself to remain open to the life of faith. That doesn't mean I put my faith in just any old thing. In addition to prayer, I have been offered all manner of vitamins and pills. They often promise a veritable fountain of youth, but I'm a bit more reticent about offering my faith in those circumstances.

A few years ago, a man came up to me after a church service. He was crying so I sort of braced myself to hear what was coming. He said, "I have the gift of healing." I replied, "Great, praise the Lord." He went on to say, "While you were speaking during the service I asked, 'Father, do you want me to pray for this man to receive his sight?' God told me to come ask you a question. Would you rather have greater spiritual sight or greater physical sight? It's your choice." I replied, "I desire greater spiritual sight." He said, "I knew you would say that," then he turned and left. A few hours later, it suddenly struck me—"What have I done?!" When I told my oldest son, Greg, he said, "Dad, you ought to go back and ask if there's a third choice."

I am not thrilled about being blind. I can say that emphatically. Yet, I know that if I live another twenty or thirty years with this handicap, it's only a drop in the bucket compared to eternity. Those of you in your forties or fifties know that you can turn around one day and realize that a decade just whizzed by. When you were in your twenties maybe you looked at people in their forties and wondered how they even walked straight. They were just so old. But now you've been married twenty years and you say, "Dear God! Where did the time go?" Our need is to understand and prepare for the life to come. We need to be men and women of character so that we will be valuable and productive for eternity. Emotionally, we scream for solutions to our problems:

"Dear God, make my wife think I'm the greatest thing ever!"

"Dear God, make my husband smarter than a stick!"

Maybe these are the problems that we're supposed to deal with. God has given us time, talent, energy, and resources. For goodness sake, we even have opposable thumbs. Surely we can grapple with some of the problems in our lives. Maybe God is waiting and watching to see how we deal with our problems. Do we become bitter or better? God wants us to grow up and to be mature. If we as earthly parents know what it means for our kids to be mature, how much more does our Heavenly Father understand and desire maturity in His children? Surely those of you with children don't want to baby sit them for the next forty years. Surely God does not want us to be spiritual babies for eternity.

Your need is the renewing of your mind in Christ Jesus. Can you renew your own mind? I don't think so. You need the power of the Holy Spirit and the wisdom of the Word to renew your mind. I don't care how much time, talent, energy, and resources you apply towards the renewing of your mind, you can't do it by yourself. God will supply our need.

So many times we beg and plead for God to solve the problems in our lives. But, as soon as He solves one problem another one will surely crop up. God asks, and expects, for us to deal with the problems in our lives. That is the path to spiritual maturity. God will meet the need of renewing our minds. God has called and commissioned His church (us!) to go into all the world and make disciples. That is our calling. Our problem is that we don't want to be committed. We don't really want to deal with it. Sometimes we'd just rather bask in the glow of uplifting worship and hope that people come knocking on our doors. I'm sorry, it simply doesn't work that way. We have to be proactive and engage our responsibilities. God will supply our needs, including the need of renewed minds.

The renewing of our mind isn't our only need. All have sinned and come short of the glory of God (Rom. 3:23). The wages of sin is death (Rom. 6:23). Have you and I sinned? Absolutely. Does that mean death? Absolutely. But, through the blood of Jesus Christ and the resurrection power of God, we are renewed into life. Resurrection life is another one of our needs. We cannot resurrect ourselves no matter how much we try. We have sinned. We will sin. We need resurrection power. That need is desperately important. We not only need a view of eternity. We need resurrection power. These needs represent our primary focus, yet so often we become consumed with daily problems. I encourage you to focus on the work God desires to achieve. Allow Him to meet your needs.

Gentlemen, we who value accomplishment have a need to be respected. This need is not the same as a renewed mind or resurrection life but it is still important. The rub is that no matter how much we apply our time, talent, energy, and resources, we cannot make people respect us. We still try. We often pursue accomplishments as a way of securing respect from others. But, accomplishment doesn't automatically equal respect. Some of the most successful people in this world are also some of the most disrespected. Respect has more to do with the way you live than what you achieve. This principle is true both in positions of lesser and greater authority. When we find ourselves in situations of power and position it's awfully tempting to please ourselves. We can even make people do what we want. But, when we choose for the best of other people not only is our ego fulfilled, other people respect us.

How does this principle translate into daily life? We are to be prophets in our homes. We often think of prophets as fore-tellers, as people who tell the future. Sometimes we even fancy ourselves fore-tellers, "If you do that one more time, you're going to be in big trouble!" But the primary responsibility of a prophet is to be a forth-teller, "This is the way. Walk in it." That's where we gain the majority of our respect.

In the Old Testament, we encounter some prophets more focused on fore-telling and some more focused on forth-telling. Sometimes respected fore-tellers didn't find their predictions coming true. In searching for an explanation, modern interpreters have described these individuals as prophets in training. However, we need to be careful when we transport that kind of concept back and forth. One of the tenets of Old Testament prophecy was reliability (Deut. 18:22). This wasn't a vocation where you scored points for trying. If you gave a false prophecy, you probably found yourself buried under a pile of rocks—one stone at a time. God didn't want false prophets walking around shooting their mouths. If that were the case, then people wouldn't have been able to trust any prophets.

I have a difficult time supposing there were Old Testament prophets in training when it came to fore-telling (I also have a difficult time supposing there are modern fore-tellers in training). But, when we speak the truth of the Word of God we can forth-tell and never miss the mark. Particular circumstances may change but God's truth never does. "This is the way. Walk in it." It might be easier to try and force compliance—"It's my way or the highway, baby!"—but that doesn't generate respect. It more likely leads to arguments about annoying problems. Pretty soon we become arguers who focus on problems and we nit-pick over the details of life. We argue that, "It better be this way." We argue about the fact that, "Everyone else has had to do it this way," or, "That's the way it was done before." We argue about this and we argue about that. Who respects an arguer? A prophet says, "This is the Wisdom of God and I'm walking in His way." A prophet forth-tells the pattern and the way of life that leads to blessing.

In addition to prophets, we are also to be priests. A priest is God's representative. A representative makes God known but is not the same as God incarnate. As a kingdom of priests we are God's representatives. We illustrate the ways of God so that others can see a reflection of God. When we fail to represent God accurately, various forms of idolatry fill the void. Idolatry isn't about the inanimate objects that people worship, perhaps some chunk of wood or a piece of metal. Idolatry is the misrepresentation of God in any way. If we misrepresent God then we open a door for idolatry. Instead of being God's priests, we become demagogues. We represent falsehood as God's truth. People don't respect demagogues. People don't respect a politician from either party who stands up to say things that are patently untrue and then claim to be a paragon of virtue. People don't respect a politician who appeals to emotion and prejudice rather than clear thinking. And yet it's easy for us to fall into that trap in our own lives. It's easy to be arguers, thinking that what we want is the way it has to be.

Not only are we to focus on the offices of prophet and priest, we are to be comprehensive godly leaders. We should be willing to lay down our lives for those we lead. There is a reason that people rejoice when the righteous are in authority and groan when the wicked rule (Prov. 29:2). People don't like to be ruled by unrighteousness. We don't gain respect by being a dictator. Do you remember when the Soviet Union fell? The statues of former dictators were attacked, abused, and shattered. The same thing happened in Baghdad not too long ago. Statues of stately figures were literally beaten with sledgehammers because people didn't respect them. They feared them.

Unfortunately, the dictator can make his way into the family home just as easily as he can ascend to political office. The household dictator assumes that respect is measured by obedience to his will. He makes bold statements and issues brash ultimatums. "You better obey me. You better respect me!" The household dictator would earn his precious respect if only he had the courage to be a godly leader, to be a priest who represents the ways of God and a prophet who forth-tells the will of God. These are the routes to respect. When you focus on the problem of your ego, when you focus on the problem of personal attention, you become an arguer, a demagogue, and a dictator. When you focus on the needs of others and the wisdom of God, you become a true leader. You become a prophet and priest in your home. Your God will supply all of your needs.

One of the great Old Testament stories is that of Jonah. I'm saddened that our culture has become rather ignorant of Biblical stories. One of the exceptions to this trend is the story of Jonah. For some reason it has endured. "Oh yeah, that story of the guy in the whale. Jonah and the whale." It's great that we remember but let's make sure we don't miss the real import of the story.

God has commissioned His prophet to go to the city of Nineveh to call them to repentance. Jonah immediately leaps up, runs down to the seashore, and boards a ship...heading in the exact opposite direction. We know that the Jews hated the Ninevites but that is only part of the reason for Jonah's behavior. Jonah reveals the real issue himself. He says, "I fled to Tarshish, for I knew that You are a gracious and compassionate God, slow to anger and abundant in loving kindness, and one who relents concerning calamity," (Jonah 4:2). From where we sit, that doesn't sound like such a bad thing. What's the issue?

Jonah had a problem. You see, Jonah belonged to a school of prophets. How do you suppose prophets gained respect? How did they reach the big time and have their egos massaged? They fore-told events that were beyond their control. The more spectacular and outlandish, the better! If you tell your prophet buddies that you're going down to Nineveh to call them to repentance, what's the payoff? What happens if Nineveh actually repents? In this case, nothing. More specifically, God will relent of the wrath that would have happened. If they don't repent then it's fire and brimstone. Then you've got destruction and devastation in the streets! If Jonah goes down there and everybody repents how does anybody really know that he heard from God? But, if you tell all of your buddies about God's wrath and then take off in the other direction, they'll be duly impressed when crispy critters fill the streets. "Whoa! What a dude, that Jonah. Don't mess with him. He'll fry ya."

Jonah is on his way to Tarshish because he wants that whole city to fry. Then everyone will know for sure that Jonah is someone to reckon with. But there's another problem, a storm. The pagan sailors are smart enough to know that something is amiss. They're up on the boat deck drawing lots to figure out what on earth is the matter. They finally figure out that it's got something to do with the Hebrew down in the hold. They go down and grab him. They bring him up and stand him on the deck. They say, "What is your problem?!" He says, "I serve a God who is loving and kind in all of His ways. He has called me to go to the city of Nineveh and call them to repentance. But I know that as sure as I go down there, they'll repent so I'm headed to Tarshish." The pagans say, "Really?!" Jonah says, "That's right. And, if you don't throw me overboard you're going to drown." It took these sailors about two seconds to figure out how to solve their problem. "See ya!" Now, Jonah has a need. How long can he tread water? Mercifully, his God supplied his need. *Sluuurp!* A whale. Isn't God good?

A couple of years ago, my wife read a report from a marine biologist who did a hypothetical study. The topic: could a human being (i.e., Jonah) actually survive in the belly of a whale? Human remains have certainly been found in the bellies of whales but that sort of misses the point. Could someone actually survive? The biologist concluded that whales in the relevant part of the ocean would have been large enough to accommodate a person in their belly. But, there would have been some very important and unpleasant considerations. First, whales are air-breathing mammals. They regularly come to the surface to breathe air. After filling with air they submerge for twenty to twenty-five minutes and their stomachs fill with water. If a person happened to be inside a whale's stomach, that person would have to find an air pocket next to the stomach lining in order to breathe. Otherwise, that person would drown. If we think about Jonah, he would have been constantly scrambling for air. Can you imagine the terror? Every time the whale submerged he would have been on the verge of drowning. The belly would have been pitch black with stuff, strange stuff, floating in the water. It would not have been nice.

The second real issue would have been that Jonah's whale, as a mammal, could not digest living flesh. Before long, that whale would have been groaning and thinking, *What did I eat back there?!* The whale's digestive system would have been pumping out gallons and gallons of stomach acid trying to digest this pesky creature. According to the marine biologist such an acid bath would not only have dissolved all of Jonah's clothing, it would also have melted his hair and bleached his skin. But wait, there's more. The acid would also have caused a rash that was constantly aggravated by the salt water.

After three days of serious indigestion this whale has finally had it. He wants nothing more than somewhere to barf! In my mind, I like to imagine that this whale found a nice little spot of beach right next to a sign reading, "Welcome to Nineveh." I like to think that a couple of families were out having a picnic when the kids say, "Daddy, look at that whale. What's that whale doing?" Daddy says, "Don't look, kids." The whale goes, *blah!* And then, out of the middle of this whale vomit stands a naked, hairless, bleached man screaming, "Repent! Repent!" How would you have responded?

The whole city of Nineveh repented, from the king on down. They repented. "When God saw their deeds, that they had turned from their wicked way, then God relented concerning the calamity which He had declared He would bring upon them. And He did not do it. But it greatly displeased Jonah and he became angry," (Jonah 3:10-4:1). Jonah went east of the city to sit on a hill. He wanted to see what God would do.

God had already told him what He was going to do. God relented. Guys, when we don't get our way, when our ego gets bruised, there's a real pressure to withdraw. Isn't it interesting? Sometimes we pull back and go sit on our own little hill to pout and see what God will do. I don't know how many times I've heard a story about a group of people at church who get so bent out of shape that they just decide to stop coming. "We'll show them. We'll see if they can make it without us. Of course, we won't give any money either." Newsflash: God doesn't need your money. If He ever needed cash, He'd just go sell one of those cows He's got on a thousand hills (cf., Psa. 50:10).

Jonah pouts, "God, death is better to me than life!" (Jonah 4:3). Jonah withdraws. He goes and he sits on a hill. Unfortunately, there's a scorching and unbearable sun. Jonah builds a shelter and God graciously causes a plant to grow. The plant provides shade for his bald, bleached head. Jonah is overjoyed by the plant (Jonah 4:6). Isn't it amazing? Jonah gets downright giddy over a silly little plant but he's absolutely furious about the salvation of an entire city!

Enter the worm. As unexpectedly as the plant sprung up, a worm comes and attacks it. The plant withers. Jonah becomes desperately angry. He says, "God, just kill me!" I must admit, I've seen the very same scene played out time and again in the local church. The particulars may not involve a plant or a worm, but I've seen angry people determined to thwart the work that God would do through church leadership. In their own way, these pouting rebels are far more excited about their own little plants than what God might have accomplished in a great city. Be careful. Don't allow yourself to thwart God's purposes because of selfish desire. God will not let you rest content with a silly plant when the stakes are so much higher. God had called Jonah to Nineveh and He wasn't about to let him substitute a plant for a city. God says, "Do you have good reason to be angry?" Jonah snaps back, "I have reason to be angry unto death, God!" Doesn't that sound just like someone who expects God to solve every little problem? God says, "Jonah, you are angry over a plant that grew up overnight and then perished. Should I not have compassion on Nineveh, the great city in which there are more than 120,000 persons who do not know the difference between their right and left hand, as well as many animals?" (Jonah 4:11). Period, end of book.

The phrase about not knowing right from left is a euphemism to denote those under the age of accountability. It describes individuals too young or incapable of being accountable. In Nineveh that number was 120,000 plus animals. The demographics suggest a total population of 450,000—500,000 people. Ancient Nineveh was an immense and incredibly wealthy metropolitan area. The city itself was surrounded by a wall with a circumference of 110 miles. Two chariots could ride side-by-side along the top of the wall. Jonah wanted to kill, literally fry, this entire place so he could win bragging rights. God says, "I don't think so, Jonah."

Just like Jonah, we can get so consumed with our problems. We focus on issues that are not true needs. All the while, we forget about the thousands of people located a mere stone's throw from the doors of our church. God says, "Don't you see the need?" People will literally die in their sin because they cannot meet their need for renewed life. Such life is not simply a matter of social, psychological, or emotional resources. The primary issue is not reducible to resource allocation. The primary issue is UNIVERSAL human need for God's new life, His resurrection and renewing power. We take so much for granted in this incredibly privileged country we inhabit. We are so blessed, yet we focus so much energy and attention on OUR problems. I challenge us to see the need of the world around us. I challenge us to be God's representatives and God's ministers to a world in need. Amen.

9

THE FOCUS OF WOMAN:
THE NEED FOR LOVE

Now the LORD saw that Leah was unloved, and He opened her womb,
but Rachel was barren. Leah conceived and bore a son and named him
Reuben, for she said, "Because the LORD has seen my affliction; surely now
my husband will love me."

~ *Genesis 29:31-32*

From Elaine:

We were visiting my parents' house in California. Roger and I, along
with our children, were sitting in the living room with my mother. We
were all a little uncomfortable because of my mother's condition. She had
contracted Multiple Sclerosis late in life, and this devastating disease had
progressed very rapidly. It was difficult for her to walk and even to talk.
Yet, that particular Sunday morning she decided that she wanted to be
at church. Since she couldn't go to her own church, we held a worship
service at my parents' home. Roger began the service with a song. We all
joined in. After the song, Roger asked if anyone had a request. In a voice
barely louder than a whisper, my mother said, "Count Your Blessings."
For a moment, we all just sat there. The title was a stark contrast to
the woman sitting before us. Her body was failing and withering.
The fact that she wanted to count her blessings was simply amazing.
Love and esteem welled up in my heart. My mind was drawn back to
my childhood years. I remembered my mother as one of the most creative

ladies in our circle of friends. During Christmas season her sewing basket was routinely "out of bounds" because of all the gifts inside. She even sewed most of my clothes, using designer patterns when I became a teenager. When family finances were tight, mom's creativity easily bridged the gap between need and want. Of all her gifts, I learned to appreciate one the most: the gift of burden bearing. Frequently, when I returned home from school, I would find my mother reading her Bible and praying at the kitchen table. She was the burden-bearer for our family through her prayers. My mother's prayerful burden bearing taught me that I was cherished and loved not only in her eyes, but also in God's eyes.

In the last chapter we focused on the difference between a problem and a need. A problem is something you can generally solve by applying your own resources. You may not want to fiddle with the seemingly endless stream of problems in your life but when you choose to apply yourself you can usually solve them. By contrast, a need is something that you cannot solve or fix by yourself, no matter how hard you try. A need is something that demands outside help. It is hugely important to recognize that God has promised to supply all of our needs (Phil. 4:19). It is so easy to focus on all of the issues that make life inconvenient, frustrating, or even mundane. When human vision extends no further than personal problems, we become shortsighted. We have a difficult time seeing past ourselves. Everyone else seems to sail through life while we struggle to keep our heads above water.

As men and women, distinct, varied, and complementary creatures, we often face distinct needs. Among those varied needs, I believe that most women have a need to be secure in the love they give and receive. The need to be loved is a powerful force. When this need is viewed as a problem to be solved in self-strength, the so-called solution can take the form of sensuality, contention, manipulation, nagging, appeasing, as well as a host of other actions. None of these "solutions" actually create the desired outcome: secure love.

The book of Genesis paints an unflinching contrast between the purposes of God and the acts of people. The book opens with a stunning portrait of God's creative Word. Creator God fashions the heavens and the earth. As the climax of this creative endeavor, God fashions the human race. Humanity represents the pinnacle of God's creation. However, when this creation is taking its first steps toward maturity, human creatures disobey God and threaten the entire created order. Having just marveled at the creative work of God, the reader of Genesis is jarringly introduced to the God of righteous judgment. God judges the man and the woman. The woman is addressed with the following curse, "I will greatly multiply your pain in childbirth, in pain you shall bring forth children" (Gen. 3:16).

Does this divine judgment represent the height of intolerance? Does the postmodern tolerance patrol have a valid gripe? Guardians of so-called tolerance claim that the God of Genesis arbitrarily lays a trip on womankind, saddling her with childbirth because she transgressed an apparently arbitrary (and oppressive) command. They claim, in short, that Eve is punished for trying to think. Frankly, that's just the wrong way to read Scripture. First, rational feminine thought is not punished. Rather, human thought is judged in relation to the ways of God. Humans are called to operate and think within the bounds of created order. Humans do not stand above creation, like God. They stand within creation and find true flourishing when they co-create with God. Human judgment is always subordinate to God's order. Second, it's not that God suddenly laid a trip on womankind by saddling her with children. The curse was a matter of pain, the fruit of human disobedience. God's creation would now struggle toward maturity in the midst of opposing forces. These consequences touched all facets of human life, from gardening to childbearing, to the structure of a godly marriage.

"Your desire shall be for your husband." That statement reflects a simple truth about the need for love. What about the following phrase? "And he shall rule over you." Let's look to the New Testament, where Paul restates this sentiment: "Be subject to one another in the fear of Christ. Wives, be subject to your own husbands, as to the Lord. For the husband is the head of the wife, as Christ also is the head of the church, He Himself being the Savior of the body... Nevertheless let each individual among you also love his own wife even as himself; and let the wife see to it that she respects her husband" (Eph. 5:21-23, 33). This passage reveals a pattern of mutual responsibility and reverence in Christian marriage. Submission is not an excuse to exclude women from positions of authority. It is certainly not an excuse for physical, emotional or sexual abuse. Submission is about love and respect, modeling Christ and the church.

Can you imagine the size of the world's population without that little addendum, "your desire..."? At some point in marriage, desire culminates in sexual intercourse, which can result in pregnancy, and then comes pain ("greatly multiplied"). Without the addendum of "desire," the world's population would probably be about twenty-seven people. Desire trumps pain, no matter how hard we kick and scream.

Back in the mid-1970s my wife and I were a young couple with three kids. We pastored a church where many of our friends were also young couples with kids. As you can imagine, all sorts of stories about children and childbirth were floating in the air. According to one of these stories, a woman from church had suffered through nearly thirty-five hours of labor. After enduring this grueling ordeal, she found herself lying on a birthing table screaming at her husband, "You will never touch me again!" Of course, the punch-line is that twenty-four months later she was lying on a similar birthing table at the same hospital screaming to the same husband, "You will never touch me again!" Desire trumps pain.

Before throwing too many stones at the Biblical narrative, we do well to hear the underlying contours of the story. The curses found in Genesis reflect truths about the human condition. We encounter the issues of desire and pain, a conflict rooted in human efforts to stand above the ways of God. Those same issues endure today. When a woman needs to be loved, it can be all too tempting to force the solution. The temptation is to focus on the problem (finding and/or fixing the right man) rather than the need (resting in God's love and provision). The desire to supplant the ways of God inevitably yields frustration and anguish.

Solomon is popularly referred to as the wisest man who ever lived (cf., 1Kings 3:12). Be that as it may, I don't think that Solomon was the most practical man who ever lived. The man may have been shrewd, but he was not smart. He indulged in hundreds of wives, many of whom practiced pagan worship contrary to God's laws, and his indulgence destroyed him (1Kings 11:3). Isn't it fascinating that the book of Proverbs, largely attributed to Solomon, talks so much about the contentious and vexing woman? However, women have not cornered the market on contention. Men can be just as contentious and vexing. Nevertheless, the picture of the contentious woman in Proverbs is striking. I define contention as: striving in human strength and wisdom to accomplish that which should be done in God's strength and wisdom. The contentious woman strives in herself to meet her need for secure love instead of trusting God to meet this need.

In Proverbs 27:15-16, Solomon offers several images to paint a picture of the contentious woman. He compares her to a continuous dripping on a rainy day. To restrain her is like restraining the wind or like trying to grasp oil. Our family lived in Oregon for many years and I became quite familiar with the phenomenon of dripping. More than once, I pulled into our garage on a rainy day and heard a little drip. I'd think, "Oh rats, I forgot to clean the gutters." If the seasons had already changed, I knew I could expect a long stretch of drippy days. The problem was really quite simple, though very vexing.

The rain was supposed to run down the roof shingles and into the gutters, but if the gutters weren't clear the water wouldn't flow into the downspout. Instead, it would drip. It wasn't a major problem. It was just a little bit of congested water that was hitting the downspout erratically—*tap, tap, tap.* When the dripping first started, I thought I'd forget about it as soon as I entered the house. I thought I probably wouldn't even be able to hear it. Unfortunately, that wasn't the case. As the afternoon and evening passed, I'd start a fire in the fireplace, maybe make some hot chocolate or popcorn but I could still hear the drip—*tap, tap, tap.* By this point the day was wearing on and it was getting closer to evening. I told myself that when I went to the back of the house later that night I wouldn't be able to hear the drip from our bedroom—*tap, tap, tap.* By about 3:00 am I was ready to cut the arm off that downspout. It was no big deal. It was just a little drip. But, positioned right between your eyes—or your ears—that little drip could drive you insane. And, just when you thought it was gone...*tap, tap, tap.* That is one of the pictures Solomon paints of contention. It seems like something so small, but it can push you over the edge.

Not only does Solomon offer the image of dripping, he says that contention is like trying to grasp oil. You know how it is if you happen to grab something covered with oil. "Oh, no!" Once you touch it, it's nearly impossible to wash off. Maybe you can relate to the following experience. Suppose you pull up to the drive-in window of your favorite burger establishment. You order a burger with fries, "and some napkins, please." After all, that kind of oily food drips like a faucet. You pull away from the drive-in window. You wrap your hamburger in a few napkins. You set your fries in the cup holder and put your drink between your legs. You take one bite of the burger and it sprays burger juice all over the place. "Oh, no!" Now you've got burger juice (mostly oil) all over your hand. You notice a stoplight and try to downshift to slow your speed. When you press the clutch, the lid slides right off your drink. Not only that, your hand knocks over the French fries as you reach for the shifter. In complete frustration you throw your burger out the window, except the window isn't open. Now you've got oil everywhere. That picture may not be exactly what Solomon had in mind but the point is the same. Contention quickly spreads beyond our grasp. Once it starts flowing, it is anything but easy to stop.

As if dripping water and spreading oil weren't enough, Solomon also says that contention is like trying to restrain the wind. Right before Elaine and I were married, we received some money to buy a bedroom set. When it was time to pick-up the bed, I borrowed an old open-air trailer with wooden slats. I pulled up to a dock at the mattress factory and handed them my invoice. Some guy slid the box springs and mattress onto the trailer. In the process he tore a small hole in the butcher paper wrapped around the mattress. He asked, "Do you want me to tape that up?" I answered, "Nah, it's no big deal. I'm just driving a few miles down the freeway." He said, "Suit yourself."

I pulled onto the freeway and discovered that rush hour was just underway. There were three lanes of traffic on my side of the road, so I pulled into the slow lane and began the drive home. I wasn't paying much attention until I noticed some unexpected motion in the rearview mirror. I looked more carefully and saw my mattress and box springs spontaneously levitate. As I continued watching, the mattress gently floated up into the air...and I was left peering at the amazing flying mattress. The amazing mattress drifted over the top of one car, then another. At this point, it began its descent and settled halfway between the median and the fast lane. Cars were swerving every-which-way trying to avoid my amazing mattress. I pulled off the road and stared at the traffic whizzing by. As I thought about darting to the other side of the highway I couldn't help but picture a headline in my mind's eye: "Bridegroom Killed Rescuing Amazing Mattress." I bravely (or foolishly) ran across three lanes of traffic and picked up my queen-sized mattress. Have you ever carried a queen-sized mattress by yourself? It's heavy! The next time you try to pick one up, remember this: a steady stream of wind propped up my mattress and gave it wings. I never imagined something like that could happen. It was just a little hole in some butcher paper. I could have blown into that hole until I was blue in the face and that mattress would never have budged. But, an unrestrained fifty mile-per-hour wind made that mattress soar like a bird.

How many times have we seen marriages that seemed so incredibly firm and grounded suddenly succumb to the winds of life? The winds of contention shake and destroy. Marriages we thought were stable and secure in love swiftly vanish before our eyes. Solomon says that it is better to live in the desert than with a contentious woman (Prov. 21:19). The surprising thing about a desert is that you can actually encounter various forms of life. Something will grow and something will live. Part of Solomon's point is that contention snuffs out any life. Nothing grows. Nothing destroys life and creativity faster than contention. Contention will destroy life in your home, in your business, or in your church. Contention. Solomon twice says it is better to live on the corner of a roof than with a contentious woman (Prov. 21:9; 25:24). The corner of a roof is where the joists come together. It's not the loveliest spot in the world but you can probably have some peace and quiet and that's part of Solomon's point. Twice he says that if there's contention, you are better off on your own. You are better off sitting on the corner of a roof. Nothing is more contagious than contention.

Ladies, when you focus on the problems surrounding your need for secure love, when you try to force the solution, that's when contention comes. That's when it becomes easy to nag. Rather than nagging you are called to esteem. Men function best (physically, emotionally, and spiritually) with the esteem of a woman. That is God's design. We've all seen it. A woman who esteems a man can make him feel like he is forty-two feet tall and walks on air. She can give a man wings. Alternately, a woman who chooses not to esteem can use a well-placed comment or a sideways glance to chop off some guy at the knees.

Esteeming requires faith. It probably isn't the most natural inclination. Your natural response is probably more along the lines of, "Who wants to esteem this guy?" Yet, when you refuse to esteem, it becomes easy to nag. You become a squeaky wheel. Who wants to love a squeaky wheel? By focusing on problems, you will never truly satisfy your need for love. Instead, you will end up with frustration. The one who lifts up and encourages is the one valued and loved.

Not only are women encouraged to esteem, they are called to be creators. Fundamentally, this is evident in the realm of human procreation but it extends much further. When I return from a speaking engagement my wife often picks me up at the airport. I ask what she'd like to do for supper. She'll say something like, "Let's just go home and have a refrigerator supper." Now, she obviously doesn't mean that we're going to eat the refrigerator. She means that she is going to find some stuff in the refrigerator and do her thing with it. If I were to look in the refrigerator I'd say, "Whoa, we're in deep trouble tonight." However, when she looks in the refrigerator she conjures up an exquisite meal. It's incredible.

This creativity has reared its head in all sorts of situations. Before I lost my vision, there was a time when my wife brought home a set of color samples for a room we decided to redecorate. She held up the different colors and told me how they all worked together and drew out different elements in different places. I just sort of scratched my head and gave an intelligent sounding, "Uh-huh." I couldn't even see what she was talking about when I could see—if you know what I mean. However, when I walked into that room when all was said-and-done I was practically speechless. I said something profound like, "I love it! How'd you do that?" She said, "I laid it out right in front of you." I just couldn't see it. She obviously could. It was simply one part of her incredible creative ability, an ability that helped build our home and family.

When a woman focuses on the problems surrounding her need for secure love, she may become a manipulator. She might let a man think he is in control, but the true power remains in her hands. She gives him just enough rope so he doesn't hurt himself and makes sure to keep all sharp objects out of the way. After all, "Somebody needs to help the boy." Tragically, manipulation never begets love. In fact, I think manipulation actually makes women angry. Deep down I believe they wish that most guys would step into their appropriate roles and join them in creative partnership. "Where are all the men?! Why do I have to raise my three children and my husband?!"

If a lady has to ask a guy to do everything, she doesn't know if he really loves her or if he's just trying to score points and look good. However, if he "just does it" she beams. Ladies, if you manipulate some guy and make him leap tall buildings for you it's just like asking him to do something. It probably makes you mad because you feel like he doesn't care. Even worse, if you can manipulate this guy then what other woman might also manipulate him? Suddenly your relationship feels pretty insecure. It is so important to focus on God as the provider of your needs. Choose to esteem. Be open to creativity.

A woman is called to be a burden-bearer. This calling applies spiritually, emotionally, and physically. Burden-bearers are not appeasers. Burden bearing is life giving and spiritually enlarging. Appeasement is life taking and spiritually shrinking. Women bear children, and they continue bearing their needs through the course of an entire life. Who do children cry for in the middle of the night? Their dad? More likely, they cry for their mother. Maybe mom pokes dad in the ribs and says, "It's your turn," but that's not the point. Kids instinctively cry for the burden-bearer. I can't tell you how many times I've awakened in the middle of the night to find my wife praying for our adult children. She still bears their burdens.

Historically speaking, the prayers of women are the seedbed for the great revivals of the church. A burden-bearer walks in a position of trust and faith, relying on God to meet her need for love. I challenge you ladies to esteem, to be creators and burden-bearers. Allow God to minister to your needs instead of trying to solve your problems by nagging, manipulating, and appeasing.

In the Biblical story of the patriarchs, Leah plays the role of the ugly duckling. Leah is Rachael's older sister. Specifically, she is the older sister with weepy eyes (Gen. 29:17), the one who nobody wants to marry. Leah's story begins when Jacob flees his home. He flees after his mother, Rebecca, manipulates his father, Isaac, and steals the inheritance blessing for her favorite son. The rightful heir, Esau, is so angry that he threatens to kill Jacob. The implication in the story is that Rebecca never sees either one of her sons after that fateful day. That is the price of her manipulation. The truly shocking thing is that Jacob is as much as seventy-four years old when this manipulation takes place! That's maternal control with a price. Rebecca loses her sons.

Jacob runs off to the land of his uncle Laban. He takes one look at Laban's daughter Rachael and says, "Wow!" Laban sets the marriage price at seven years of labor. Jacob says, "No problem!" According to the story, those seven years passed as quickly as one day. They seemed like nothing because Jacob's heart was set on Rachael. In contrast, imagine how those seven years felt for Leah. She was the oldest sister. According to tradition, she was supposed to be married first (Gen. 29:26), but now the youngest sister was betrothed. Nagging questions from other people were surely floating in the air, "Leah, don't you have a man yet?"

The wedding day finally comes. Near sunset, when the celebration is reaching its climax, Laban scoots up next to Leah and says, "Get your stuff, girl." She says, "What?"

"Get your stuff."

"Why?"

"I'm going to take you to Jacob's tent."

"What?!"

"That's right. The oldest is always married first. You're going to Jacob's tent tonight."

"But, Dad!"

"Get your stuff, girl."

She knew exactly what Laban was up to. He was going to turn off all the nightlights in that tent and make sure that Jacob was real happy. But, the next morning when Jacob rolled over expecting to see his beautiful Rachael and found Leah, you could have heard the scream for two blocks. "Laban! Laban, what have you done to me?!"

How would you have felt, ladies? Leah didn't choose this situation. She was railroaded into it. Suddenly she found herself married and her husband barely knew she existed. On top of everything else, Jacob cut a deal for another seven years labor so he could win the hand of beloved Rachael. It could not have been any clearer: Leah was unloved.

"Now the LORD saw that Leah was unloved, and He opened her womb, but Rachel was barren," (Gen. 29:31). Leah bore a son. The greatest blessing for a woman in the ancient Mid East was to bear a child. Moreover, the greatest blessing in childbirth was to bear a male child. The birth of a son meant that God's blessing was upon a woman. "Leah conceived and bore a son and named him Reuben, for she said, 'Because the LORD has seen my affliction; surely now my husband will love me'" (Gen. 29:32).

"See, husband! See what I've done for you! Can't you see?" Many women today make the same cry. "Don't you see what I've done? Don't you see how important you are in my life? Don't you see?"

But still she was unloved. "Then she conceived again and bore a son and said, 'Because the LORD has heard that I am unloved, He has therefore given me this son also.' So she named him Simeon" (Gen. 29:33).

"Hear me! Hear me, husband! Don't you hear how much I do? Don't you hear how committed and faithful I am? Hear me!" Perhaps your cry is the cry of Leah. Perhaps all you hear is a flippant response. "Well, that's just the little woman talking. What does she know?"

"Don't you see?! Don't you hear?!"

And still she was unloved. "She conceived again and bore a son and said, 'Now this time my husband will become attached to me, because I have born him three sons.' Therefore he was named Levi" (Gen. 29:34).

"Husband, don't you know that we're attached? Don't you know that we're a part of each other? Don't you know?" Attachment is so much more than those moments of sexual intimacy. Attachment is a matter of enduring desire (Gen. 3:16). We live in a culture all too casual about the proverbial one-night stand. Many have indulged in a youthful fling and are still dealing with the consequences years later. "We're attached, husband. Don't you see? Don't you realize?"

And still she was unloved. "And she conceived again and bore a son and said, 'This time I will praise the Lord.' Therefore she named him Judah" (Gen. 29:35). After the birth of this fourth son, Leah seemed to make a breakthrough. She seemed to reach a point of recognition. The truth was that no matter what she did (e.g., bearing four sons) or no matter how much she screamed she could never make Jacob love her. She couldn't fix that need. Her response after the birth of Judah was wonderfully appropriate, "This time I will praise the Lord."

Unfortunately, that wasn't Leah's final response. In the following narrative a birthing duel ensues between Leah and Rachel. Each of them competes for the place of honor, the honor achieved through childbirth. Leah again grasps and strains for the place of privilege (Gen. 30:20), only to find herself bested by Rachel (Gen. 30:22-24). Did she ever return to a posture of praise? Did Leah allow God to meet her need to be loved?

How does Leah ultimately fare in the pages of Scripture? Near the end of Genesis, Jacob blesses his sons and charges them with instructions for his burial. Jacob will be buried in the cave of his ancestors. His bones belong next to the bones of Abraham and his wife Sarah. His bones belong next to the bones of Isaac and his wife Rebekah. His bones belong next to the bones of his own wife Leah (Gen. 49:31). This is the cave where Jacob belongs, and it is the cave where he buried Leah who died before him. Leah's final resting place was a place of honor. She, not Rachel, was named with the great ancestors of Israel. There was a life-history behind that burial location. Scripture may be silent on Leah's later life, but there would surely be no mention of her at the time of Jacob's death unless she was remembered with honor and esteem. She chose to praise the Lord, however flawed or imperfect, and she was loved.

10

CONCLUSION:
I DARE YOU TO DO IT AGAIN!

Then I went down to the potter's house, and there he was, making something on the wheel. But the vessel that he was making of clay was spoiled in the hand of the potter; so he remade it into another vessel, as it pleased the potter to make... "Can I not, O house of Israel, deal with you as this potter does?' declares the Lord. "Behold, like the clay in the potter's hand, so are you in My hand."

~ Jeremiah 18:3-4,6

There once was a man who excelled in business. He reached the pinnacle of his profession, earning a large salary and accumulating vast possessions. He knew both status and wealth. Without warning, his fortunes suddenly changed. His company was purchased and his position was cut. To make matters worse, his lucrative investments crashed when the market hit a slump. After being on top of the world, he suddenly found himself scraping the bottom of the barrel. He lived in a borrowed apartment and could barely afford a broken down car. In addition to his financial woes, his wife was in the hospital dying of cancer, his son was in the county jail on drug charges, and his daughter—pregnant and unmarried—was sharing an apartment with her latest lover.

One Sunday night, he realized that everything was gone. He couldn't even afford to buy groceries. He had $5.00. That was it. His vast fortune had whittled down to a single five-dollar bill. *Enough!* He decided he was going to put an end to his misery. He got in his rickety car and began looking for a bridge. He was going to jump. On his way, he happened to pass a small church. He noticed a few lights inside and decided to make peace with God before he took his life. Much to his surprise, he got more than he bargained for. He walked right into a church service that changed his life. He found himself gripped by the Gospel and filled with new life. As he approached the pastor after the service, he heard a voice in his heart warmly asking, "What do you have in your pocket?" The man answered, "A five dollar bill." The voice said, "Give it to this pastor." The man replied, "But God, it's all I have left!" The voice responded, "Do you really think five dollars is going to make a difference in your life? Give it to the man!" He handed the pastor his five-dollar bill and walked out the door.

About a year later, again on a Sunday night, the man returned to the little church. Before the service began, he approached the pastor and asked, "Do you remember me?" The pastor said, "Sure I do. This is a small church. You came in here about a year ago looking pretty rough. You prayed at the altar after the service and then handed me a five dollar bill on your way out the door." The man said, "That's right. Could I share my story with the church?" The pastor said yes.

Near the end of the service, the pastor invited the man up front to share his story. The man said, "About a year ago I decided to kill myself. Before ending my life, I came to this church on a whim to make peace with God. I was a total wreck, but God got a hold of me in this church and changed my heart. I made a commitment to Jesus before I left, and on my way out the door God told me to give my last five-dollar bill to the pastor. Reluctantly, I did so. After leaving the church, I went to the hospital and prayed for my wife who was dying of cancer. Now, a year later, she is totally cancer free." The congregation exclaimed, "Praise God!" The man continued, "The next morning I went to the county jail and prayed with my son. He is now clean and sober and preparing for ministry. After praying with my son, I went to the apartment where my pregnant daughter and her boyfriend were living. We prayed together. One year later, they are now a loving family." Again, the congregation shouted, "Praise God!" The man said, "A few days later I ran into a friend who proposed an investment opportunity. Even though I had no money, he included me in the venture. In a short time, we were both multimillionaires. My wife and I have spent much of this past year traveling the world, donating thousands of dollars to help with various missions projects." Once again, everyone in the church exclaimed, "Praise God!"

On the way back to his seat, an elderly gentleman gripped the man's arm and looked him straight in the eyes. With surprising strength the old man said, "I dare you to give it all away again!"

Young or old, male or female, rich or poor, this is the challenge we face. In both trial and triumph, do we recognize that God is the Potter and we are the clay? May we come to know ourselves as the Potter's vessels. May we find our vision, endurance, passion and focus in His loving hands.